"Fresh From Central Market"

COOKBOOK

"Fresh From Central Market"

COOKBOOK

Favorite Recipes from the Standholders of the Nation's Oldest Farmers Market, Central Market in Lancaster, Pennsylvania

By *The New York Times* Bestselling Author
Phyllis Pellman Good

Good Books

Intercourse, PA 17534
800/762-7171
www.GoodBooks.com

To all who have given life
to Central Market –
its standholders, its customers,
its advocates throughout the region

Acknowledgments

In addition to recipes from Central Market's current standholders (and a few customers), this book contains several favorite recipes from earlier standholders. These recipes first appeared in one of two previously published collections, either *The Central Market Cookbook* or *Recipes from Central Market* (both published by Good Books).

All photography © 2009 by Jeremy Hess Photographers / JH

Design by Cliff Snyder

Library of Congress Cataloging-in-Publication Data
Good, Phyllis Pellman,
 Fresh from Central Market cookbook : favorite recipes from the standholders of the nation's oldest farmers market, Central Market in Lancaster, Pennsylvania / Phyllis Pellman Good.
     p. cm.
 Includes index.
 ISBN 978-1-56148-678-6 (softcover : alk. paper) 1. Cookery. I. Central Market (Lancaster, Pa.) II. Title.
 TX714.G65 2009
 641.5--dc22   2009034077

Table of Contents

About This Cookbook—
and the Place from Which It Came

Just off Penn Square in downtown Lancaster, Pennsylvania, stands the oldest, continually operating farmers market in the United States—*Central Market*. The Market is both a stunning building and a three-times-a-week event.

It is an architectural wonder with its gracefully historic character. It is also a throbbing and enduring marketplace where truck farmers, devoted cooks, skillful bakers, and local butchers bring their beloved local, home-prepared products to their customers every Tuesday, Friday, and Saturday.

Central Market is supported by its residential neighbors, by the business and professional workers who share its streets, and by all the loyals who drive in from greater Lancaster and even nearby states to shop its busy aisles.

What brings the customers? What keeps the standholders? What sustains the remarkable life in this place at the heart of Lancaster?

There are answers: Local food that can't be resisted because it is carefully grown and produced by knowledgeable hands. Spirited standholders who understand their work as artisans. Devoted customers who know that going to Market is always worth the trip, the earlier in the day, the better. A city and a Market Trust who recognize the treasure with which they have been entrusted and who continually interpret (and re-interpret) the Market's charter—and intervene when it is challenged.

Those who bring their fresh bounty to Market, and those who line up to take it away, know good food. They are all attuned to the seasons. They understand texture and flavor. They enjoy the robust and the subtle. It is these "experts"—who work with the truck-patch-grown, the home-baked, the hand-prepared—who have offered their own favorite recipes for this cookbook.

Some of these recipes call for products the standholders produce and sell; some of the recipes are for making well rooted traditional dishes; some are simply personal favorites of the standholders. As a collection, *Fresh from Central Market Cookbook* mirrors the mix that Central Market is—the historic and novel; the foods of those who settled in Lancaster long ago, and those who have made their home in southeastern Pennsylvania more recently; startlingly simple dishes, and multi-stepped productions.

I am grateful to the many standholders who took time away from their market-tending and market preparation to put their recipes in readable form for this book. Michael Ervin, Market Manager, and Susan Glouner, Standholder Association President, made many connections for me. Steve Scott did considerable research on the Market's history and wrote much of the historical material. Kate Good added more current facts.

Central Market offers its irresistible food when you visit its brick-walled aisles—or when you prepare any of these choice recipes!

Phyllis Pellman Good

Central Market
Lancaster, Pennsylvania

Lancaster's Central Market becomes a vitally active place of commerce and friendship every Tuesday, Friday, and Saturday. Then, with dependable regularity, trucks, vans, and station wagons crowd the streets and alleys surrounding the Romanesque building. Before daybreak, Market standholders "set up"—unpacking and displaying their wares that attract a steady stream of customers from far and near.

It is a tradition for standholders and Market shoppers alike—"Once it's in your blood," they say, "you can't stay away." For what compares with fresh tomatoes and herbs gathered just a few hours earlier, with pecan rolls and cherry crumb pies made only yesterday, with meat prepared in nearby smokehouses, and with seeing friends at least once a week?

Central Market was built in 1889. But the habit of going to market is older still. When Andrew and James Hamilton planned the town in 1730, they provided for a market place, measuring 120 feet square.

When Lancaster was incorporated as a borough in 1742, its charter from George II of England established the market practice: "And we do further grant for us, our heirs and successors ... to have, hold, and keep ... two markets in each week." Already in 1744 a visitor in the town remarked, "They have a good market in this town, well filled with provisions of all kinds and prodigiously cheap." A few decades later (in 1776) a British officer paroled in Lancaster remarked, "Food is very plentiful. The markets abound with most excellent cyder and provisions."

The first Lancaster farmers market was held outdoors, but by 1757 a market house had been constructed, although it was probably a rather primitive structure. In 1763 part of the market house was reserved for the storage of three fire engines.

The city was soon under pressure to erect a larger and more substantial building for market. For a while, the farmers market shared a building with City Hall and a Masonic Lodge. Before long, this proved to be an inadequate solution. But a shortage of nearby available property made it nearly impossible to meet the demands of vendors and customers alike.

The Curb Market and Neighborhood Markets

Finally, in the 1820s, in order to relieve the situation, farmers were permitted to back their wagons up to the curbs along the streets and sell their goods directly from their vehicles or temporary stands. This gathering of sellers became known as the "curb market." It was an outgrowth of Central Market, but it developed as a distinct entity.

After the First World War, motor vehicles began replacing horse-drawn wagons at the curb market. Eventually, increased auto traffic through the city caused the curb market to be impractical and unsafe. On January 1, 1927, the city decreed that this colorful institution would come to an end. The standholders were offered space in the Southern Market.

In the late 1800s, as the city was scrambling to provide adequate space for its marketers, a series of neighborhood markets opened throughout Lancaster. In fact, at least eight other farmers markets once operated within Lancaster. It was not unusual for standholders to sell at several different markets on different days of the week.

These were the markets, their years of operation, and their locations:

The Curb Market, 1818-1927.

The Northern Market, 1872-1953, on the northwest corner of Queen and Walnut Streets.

The Eastern Market, 1882-1918, on the southeast corner of King and Shippen Streets.

The Western Market, 1882-1920, on the southeast corner of Orange and Pine Streets.

The Southern Market, 1888-1986, on the southwest corner of Queen and Vine Streets.

The Fulton Market, 1907-1971, on Plum Street, between Frederick Street and Hand Avenue.

The Arcade Market, 1927-1965, between Orange and Marion Streets, and between Prince and Market Streets.

The West End Market, 1954-1985, on the northwest corner of Lemon and Mary Streets.

It was in 1889 that the current Central Market building was erected. Very little change was made to the market house until 1973. Then, as part of an urban renewal project, the city began major restoration work on the structure. Because the Market was by then listed on the National Register of Historic Places, the Department of Housing and Urban Development provided a grant of $402,000, and the city supplied matching funds.

Under the direction of architect S. Dale Kaufman, stands were relocated to provide more aisle space, and a new underground electrical system and sewers were installed. Despite considerable inconvenience to the standholders and shoppers, the mayor announced that the Market would stay open during the whole renovation process in order to keep a two-century-old tradition alive. The refurbished market house was officially dedicated on March 21, 1975.

Most stalls or units were now six feet long, with a few being nine feet or an irregular length. In the new arrangement the stands requiring plumbing facilities for cleanup (fresh meat, fish, etc.) were limited to the rows along three of the walls and rows B and C on the west side.

One long-standing tradition changed in the remodeled market house: the fish stands were relocated inside the building. Previously, fish was sold only outside at stands along the north side of the market house. Adequate ventilation in the new Central Market took care of a potential odor problem.

Periodic repairs to the market building are made by the city of Lancaster. In 2008, Central Market Trust, the 13-member board of directors that oversees the Market, launched a capital campaign to repair the building's roof, gutters, and mechanical systems. As with all changes to the building, these renovations were carefully considered with a view toward preserving the historic architecture and character of the Market.

A tiny restaurant that occupied the southeast corner of the Market was done away with during the remodeling in the 1970s. While many of the current stands sell ready-to-eat foods, the Trust works to retain the *marketplace* character of Central Market, rather than having it become an *eating* place. Many lunchtime shoppers like to buy a small quantity of meat at one stand and rolls at another stand in order to make their own sandwiches while at the Market.

There is no doubt that Central Market has become one of Lancaster's main attractions. Despite a deluge of out-of-town visitors, City Council has made a concentrated effort to keep the Market a true farmers market and not one that views visitors as its primary customers. The regulations specify that the stands "be used solely for the sale of food products and farm-produced goods…" Several stands established before the ruling went into effect continue to sell craft and souvenir-type items. No new stands will be granted this privilege.

Market Auctions and Rents

Standholders pay a yearly rent for the stalls they occupy. When a standholder wants to discontinue business at the Market, a new standholder is chosen by the Central Market Trust after going through a stringent application process. The Trust evaluates prospective standholders' business plans, as well as the type of merchandise they hope to sell. The Trust is particularly interested in new tenants that will sell fresh and local foods.

When a standholder dies, the market stand may be passed to a spouse or child, if approved by the Trust. Several market stands are currently occupied by descendants of families who have had stands for three, four, and even five generations.

The Market Manager

In the wee hours of every Tuesday, Friday, and Saturday morning a lone figure's footsteps echo down the brick sidewalks leading to the Central Market building. The man goes to the various entrances, unlocking the large metal doors, just ahead of the trucks bringing fruits, vegetables, meat, fish, and baked goods. The man with the keys is the Market Manager. It is his responsibility to see that all runs smoothly within the Market.

In 1870 a city ordinance was passed which states, "...The Mayor shall appoint a Market Master, whose duty it shall be to attend the market during market hours, and such other times as shall be necessary...; he shall prevent the sale of or exposing to sale all unsound and unwholesome provisions..." The responsibility of keeping the Market clean and the removal of snow were also given to the Market Master, now known as the Market Manager.

The Market belongs to and reflects the Lancaster community. The quality that is Central Market is expressed not only in the magnificent building which houses it, but also in the food and wares that are sold there—much of it home-grown and home-prepared from Lancaster's truck farms, home bakeries, and butcher shops. May it continue as it was designated in the city of Lancaster's charter: "to have, hold, and keep...market...in every week of the year forever!"

Market Days and Hours

Central Market is open from 6:00 a.m. to 4:00 p.m. on Tuesdays and Fridays, and from 6:00 a.m. to 2:00 p.m. on Saturdays. That schedule changes if Christmas or New Year's Day falls on Tuesday, Friday, and Saturday. An extra market day may be added during special holiday weeks. Central Market is located just off the northwest corner of Penn Square in the center of Lancaster City.

SALADS

That Good Salad

Susan Stoeckl
SUSAN'S SECRET GARDEN

Makes 8–10 servings
Prep. Time: 15–20 minutes

¾ cup vegetable oil

¼ cup fresh lemon juice

2 garlic cloves, minced

½ tsp. salt

½ tsp. pepper

2 bunches (1 lb. each) romaine lettuce, torn

2 cups chopped tomatoes

1 cup shredded Swiss cheese

⅔ cup slivered, toasted almonds, *optional*

½ cup grated Parmesan cheese

8 bacon strips, fried and crumbled

1 cup Caesar salad croutons

1. In a jar, with tight-fitting lid, combine oil, lemon juice, garlic, salt, and pepper. Cover tightly and shake well. Chill until needed.

2. In a large salad bowl, toss lettuce, tomatoes, Swiss cheese, almonds if you wish, Parmesan cheese, and bacon.

3. Just before serving, shake dressing and pour over salad. Toss.

4. Top with croutons and serve immediately.

Green Bean Salad with Corn, Basil, and Black Olives

Janelle Glick
LANCASTER GENERAL WELLNESS PARTNERSHIP

Makes 8 servings
Prep. Time: 1 hour

2 lbs. fresh green beans, trimmed and cut into 1½" lengths

3 ears corn, husked and silked

half a small red bell pepper, finely chopped

1 small red onion, finely chopped

⅔ cup black olives, preferably salt-cured, halved, and pitted

⅓ cup chopped fresh basil

¼ cup extra-virgin olive oil

3 Tbsp. balsamic vinegar

3 Tbsp. lemon juice

2 cloves garlic, minced

hot sauce, such as Tabasco, to taste

salt to taste

freshly ground pepper to taste

1. Put a large pot of water on to boil. Fill another large pot half-full with ice water.

2. Blanch about half the green beans in boiling water just until crisp-tender, about 1-2 minutes.

3. Remove with slotted spoon and plunge into ice water.

4. Drain and transfer to a large bowl. Repeat with remaining beans.

5. Return water to boil and add ears of corn. Blanch until crisp-tender, about 3 minutes.

6. Drain and immediately plunge into ice water. Drain and cut off kernels.

7. Add corn to beans in bowl, along with bell pepper, onion, olives, basil, oil, vinegar, lemon juice, and garlic.

8. Toss to mix well.

9. Season with hot sauce, salt, and pepper.

TIP

To ease preparation time, do Steps 1–6 a day before serving the salad. Store green beans and corn in separate plastic bags lined with paper towels. Refrigerate until ready to use.

Mandarin Orange Salad

Ethel Stoner
STONER'S VEGETABLES

Makes 8-10 servings
Prep. Time: 10 minutes ❦ *Cooking Time: 10 minutes* ❦ *Cooling Time: 5 minutes*

Dressing:

¼ cup olive, *or* vegetable, oil

2 Tbsp. snipped fresh parsley

2 Tbsp. sugar

2 Tbsp. vinegar

½ tsp. salt

dash of pepper

2 Tbsp. mandarin orange juice, *optional*

6–8 drops hot sauce, *optional*

Salad:

½ cup sliced almonds

3 Tbsp. sugar

1 lb. salad greens

2 green onions, thinly sliced, *optional*

1 cup celery, chopped

11-oz. can mandarin oranges, drained, juice reserved for Dressing

1. Shake Dressing ingredients together in covered jar. Refrigerate until ready to use.

2. Cook almonds and sugar over low heat in heavy skillet, stirring constantly, until sugar is melted and almonds are coated. Set aside to cool.

3. Just before serving, layer salad greens, onions, celery, and orange slices into large salad bowl.

4. Drizzle dressing over top.

5. Add almonds and toss all ingredients together. Serve immediately.

Greens 'n Fruit Salad

Jim and Linda Kreider
COUNTRY MEADOWS

Makes 6 servings ❧ *Prep. Time: 20 minutes*

Salad:

6 cups torn salad greens

2 medium navel oranges, peeled and sectioned

1 cup halved red seedless grapes

½ cup golden raisins

¼ cup red onion, sliced thin

¼ cup toasted almonds, sliced

4 bacon strips, cooked and crumbled

Dressing:

½ cup mayonnaise

¼ cup orange juice

½ cup honey

2 Tbsp. grated orange peel

1. In large bowl combine all Salad ingredients.

2. In a smaller bowl whisk together Dressing ingredients.

3. At the table, pass Dressing along with Salad. (Refrigerate any remaining Dressing for your next salad.)

NOTE
_____

This is our traditional Christmas Salad.

Warm Raspberry Salad

Cindy Cover
MARION CHEESE

Makes 6–8 servings
Prep. Time: 5 minutes ❧ *Cooking Time: 5 minutes*

1 medium head romaine, *or* mix of salad greens

1 small can sliced water chestnuts, drained

½ tsp. cracked black pepper

3 Tbsp. walnut oil

1. Wash and tear salad greens. In a large bowl, combine with water chestnuts and season with pepper. Chill until ready to serve.

2. Heat walnut oil in large skillet. Add almonds and sauté over high heat 1–2 minutes.

½ cup slivered almonds

¾ lb. fresh mushrooms, cleaned and sliced

¼ cup raspberry vinegar

NOTE

This dish allows salad to be a more substantial part of a meal. It is tart and full of textures.

3. Add sliced mushrooms and sauté another 2 minutes.

4. Add raspberry vinegar and stir briefly.

5. Pour dressing over chilled greens and toss. Serve immediately.

Strawberry Salad

Becky Friedrich
THOMAS PRODUCE

Makes 6–8 servings
Prep. Time: 25 minutes   Chilling Time: 2 hours

⅓ cup olive oil

⅓ cup raspberry vinegar

3 Tbsp. sugar

½ tsp. Tabasco sauce

½ tsp. salt

¼ tsp. ground pepper

½ tsp. cinnamon

6 cups, *or* 2 bunches, your choice of lettuce

11-oz. can mandarin oranges, drained

1 pint strawberries, stemmed and quartered

1 small red onion, thinly sliced, *or* 1 bunch scallions, chopped

½ cup pecans, toasted and chopped

1 avocado, peeled and sliced

1. In a jar combine olive oil, vinegar, sugar, Tabasco sauce, salt, pepper, and cinnamon. Shake well. Refrigerate 2 hours.

2. Just before serving, in a large bowl combine lettuce, oranges, strawberries, onion, pecans, and sliced avocado.

3. Drizzle half the dressing on salad. Toss gently.

4. Pour remaining dressing in small pitcher.

5. Serve salad with extra dressing on the side.

TIP

Prepare the salad just before serving to prevent greens from wilting.

Crunchy Pear and Celery Salad

Ruth Thomas
THOMAS PRODUCE

Makes 6 servings
Prep. Time: 25 minutes ❧ *Chilling Time: 15 minutes*

4 stalks celery, trimmed and cut in half crosswise

2 Tbsp. cider, pear, raspberry, *or* other fruit vinegar

2 Tbsp. honey

¼ tsp. salt

2 ripe pears, preferably Bartlett *or* Anjou, diced

1 cup white cheddar cheese, finely chopped

½ cup toasted pecans, chopped

freshly ground black pepper

6 large lettuce leaves

1. Soak celery in bowl of ice water for 15 minutes.

2. Drain and pat dry. Cut into ½" pieces.

3. In a large bowl whisk together vinegar, honey, and salt.

4. Add pears. Gently stir to coat.

5. Add celery, cheese, and pecans. Stir to combine.

6. Season with pepper.

7. Divide lettuce leaves among 6 plates.

8. Place a scoop of salad on top of each leaf.

9. Serve at room temperature or chilled.

Apple and Celery Salad

Trish Hillegas
SWEETHEARTS OF LANCASTER COUNTY

Makes 3-4 servings ❧ *Prep. Time: 20 minutes*

2 cups diced apples

2 Tbsp. lemon juice

1 cup sour cream

3-oz. pkg. cream cheese, softened

2 cups diced celery

½ cup chopped almonds, *or* pecans

lettuce leaves

1. In a medium-sized bowl, mix chopped apples with lemon juice to prevent browning. Refrigerate until needed.

2. In a small bowl, mix sour cream and cream cheese together until well blended.

3. Place celery and nuts in good-sized mixing bowl.

4. Drain apples. Stir in with celery and nuts.

5. Fold sour cream and cream cheese mixture into apples, celery, and nuts.

6. Serve over lettuce leaves.

Layered Fruit Salad

Margie Shaffer
S. CLYDE WEAVER, INC.

Makes 8 servings ⚘ *Prep. Time: 25–30 minutes*
Cooking Time: 8 minutes ⚘ *Cooling Time: 10 minutes* ⚘ *Chilling Time: 3 hours*

½ cup orange juice
¼ cup lemon juice
¼ cup packed brown sugar
½ tsp. grated orange peel
½ tsp. grated lemon peel
1 cinnamon stick
2 cups pineapple chunks
1½ cups red grapes
2 medium bananas, sliced
1 large seedless orange, peeled and sectioned
1½ cups sliced strawberries, *divided*
1 kiwi, peeled and sliced
mint sprigs, *optional*

1. In medium saucepan, combine first 6 ingredients.

2. Bring to a boil. Reduce heat. Simmer uncovered 5 minutes.

3. Remove from heat and cool completely.

4. While sauce is cooling, layer fruit in glass serving bowl in order given, using only 1 cup strawberries. (Reserve remaining strawberries for garnish.)

5. Remove cinnamon stick from sauce. Pour sauce over fruit. Do not stir.

6. Garnish salad with a few strawberries on top and sprigs of mint, if you wish.

7. Cover and chill for at least 3 hours before serving.

Abundantly Herbed Potato Salad

Regine Ibold
REGINE'S COFFEE

Makes 12-16 servings
Prep. Time: 45 minutes ✿ *Marinating Time: 30 minutes*

Dressing:

¾ cup extra virgin olive oil

3 Tbsp. tarragon vinegar

¼ tsp. salt

fresh ground pepper

Salad:

4 lbs. red-skinned or Yukon Gold boiling potatoes, ping-pong-ball-sized, steamed until just tender and quartered

¾ cup scallions, thickly sliced

⅓ cup flat-leaf parsley, minced

⅓ cup fresh tarragon, minced

2 Tbsp. fresh dill, minced

2 Tbsp. fresh celery leaves, minced

1 lb. green snap beans, steamed and cut in 1" lengths

4 hard-boiled eggs, coarsely chopped

1. Whisk oil with vinegar, salt, and pepper.

2. Place ½ cup of dressing in a large bowl. Add potatoes, scallions, parsley, tarragon, dill, and celery leaves. Add beans and eggs.

3. Marinate at room temperature for at least 30 minutes.

4. Add remaining dressing and additional salt, if necessary.

Blue Cheese Potato Salad

Kathleen Pianka
MARION CHEESE

Makes 6–8 servings
Prep. Time: 20 minutes ❧ Cooking Time: 15 minutes ❧ Chilling Time: 3–4 hours

2 lbs. new red potatoes, cut into quarters
½ tsp. salt, *or more if needed*
2 celery ribs, chopped
3 scallions, chopped
½ cup sour cream
½ cup mayonnaise
¼ cup Stilton, *or your favorite blue cheese, crumbled*
¼ cup fresh parsley, chopped
pepper to taste

1. Cook potatoes in good-sized saucepan in boiling water. Cook for about 15 minutes, or until fork-tender but not falling apart.

2. Drain well. Salt potatoes while hot.

3. Allow potatoes to cool to room temperature in large mixing bowl.

4. Meanwhile, prepare celery and scallions.

5. Fold remaining ingredients into cooled potatoes.

6. Taste and add more salt if needed.

7. The Salad is best if its flavors can blend for several hours in the fridge before serving.

My grandparents brought produce to the old curb market. They would get up at one o'clock in the morning and drive their horse-drawn market wagon from Mt. Nebo (in southern Lancaster County) into the city of Lancaster. I remember how well kept the market wagon was. They would park along the curb and sell produce from the wagon.

— MIRIAM HESS, Frank Weaver Greenhouses

Sausage and Potato Salad

Susan Glouner
TURKEY LADY

Makes 2-4 servings
Prep. Time: 30 minutes ❧ Cooking Time: 25 minutes

¾ lb. red potatoes

6 ozs. rope turkey sausage

2 Tbsp. balsamic vinegar

1 Tbsp. Dijon mustard

3 Tbsp. chicken broth, *divided*

1 Tbsp., plus 1 tsp., olive oil, *divided*

½ cup red onion, diced

1 cup canned red kidney beans, rinsed and drained

salt and freshly ground pepper

½ cup fresh parsley, chopped

half a small head romaine lettuce

medium-sized tomato

salt and freshly ground pepper

1. Wash potatoes but do not peel.

2. Cut into ½" pieces.

3. Place in medium-sized saucepan and cover with cold water.

4. Cover and simmer 12–15 minutes, or until tender.

5. Cut sausage into ½"-thick slices.

6. Sauté in skillet for 10 minutes or until cooked through.

7. Whisk vinegar and mustard in a large serving bowl.

8. Whisk in 2 Tbsp. chicken broth and 1 Tbsp. olive oil.

9. Add onion and beans.

10. Season with salt and pepper to taste.

11. When potatoes are no longer hot, drain and add, still warm, to bowl.

12. Add cooked sausage, parsley, and more salt and pepper if you wish.

13. Wash lettuce leaves and place in a layer on serving platter.

14. Spoon salad onto lettuce.

15. Wash and cut tomato into thin wedges. Arrange tomato wedges over salad.

16. Mix remaining chicken broth and olive oil and spoon over tomato.

Henner's Bratwürst with Potato Salad

Henner and Heidi Steinle
THE GERMAN DELI

Makes 4 servings ❦ *Prep. Time: 30–40 minutes*
Cooking Time: 35–45 minutes ❦ *Cooling Time: 10 minutes* ❦ *Marinating Time: 1 hour*

2 lbs. potatoes, peeled or unpeeled

2 medium-sized onions

5 Tbsp. vegetable oil, *divided*

1 cup water

5–6 tsp. herb vinegar

1 beef bouillon cube, *or* 1 Tbsp. beef bouillon powder

1 tsp. salt

¼–½ tsp. pepper, according to your taste preference

12 small bratwursts

bunch of fresh chives

1. Wash potatoes. Place in stockpot, cover with water, and cook 20 minutes, covered, or until tender but not falling apart.

2. Remove from pot, rinse, and let cool.

3. Cut into thick slices.

4. Peel onions and chop.

5. Heat 1 Tbsp. oil in large skillet. Sauté onions until soft.

6. Add 1 cup water, vinegar, and bouillon.

7. Bring to simmer and cook 5 minutes.

8. In a small bowl, mix 2 Tbsp. oil with salt and pepper.

9. Pour over potatoes. Stir together thoroughly. Marinate for at least 1 hour.

10. Sauté bratwurst in large skillet in 2 Tbsp. oil until browned.

11. Wash chives and cut into small pieces. Mix into potato salad. Taste and add more salt and pepper if you wish.

12. Place potato salad in center of large platter. Surround with bratwurst and serve.

Nacho Salad

Thelma Thomas
SPRING GLEN

Makes 1-2 servings ❦ *Prep. Time: 10-15 minutes*

1 cup lettuce, shredded
⅓ cup fresh tomato, chopped
1 Tbsp. green onions, sliced
½ cup cottage cheese
3 Tbsp. salsa
2 Tbsp. cheddar cheese, shredded
1¼ cups tortilla chips
2 Tbsp. taco sauce, *optional*

1. Layer ingredients in salad bowl(s) as follows: lettuce, tomato, green onion, cottage cheese, salsa, shredded cheese.

2. Crush tortilla chips and scatter on top of salad.

3. Top with taco sauce if you wish.

NOTE

This is my husband's and my favorite Sunday evening supper.

Chicken Romaine Salad

Jim and Linda Kreider
COUNTRY MEADOWS

Makes 8-10 servings
Prep. Time: 30 minutes ❦ *Cooking Time: 10 minutes*

Salad:
3 Tbsp. butter, melted
1 cup broken pecans
½ tsp. salt
½ lb. chicken breasts, cooked and cut in chunks
7 cups torn romaine lettuce
1 cup seedless red grapes
½ cup dried cranberries
½ cup shredded cheddar cheese

1. Pour butter into 9" × 13" baking pan.

2. Stir in pecans and salt.

3. Bake at 350° for 10 minutes, stirring twice.

4. Remove from oven and set aside.

5. In a large bowl combine remaining Salad ingredients.

6. Sprinkle roasted pecans into Salad.

Creamy Dijon Dressing:

¼ cup prepared mustard

½ cup mayonnaise

½ cup orange juice

¼ cup honey

¼ tsp. celery seed

7. Place all Dressing ingredients together in jar with tight-fitting lid. Shake until well combined.

8. Stir Dressing into Salad just before serving.

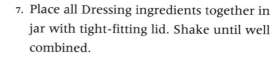

Grilled Chicken Salad

Dawn Mellinger
ROHRER FAMILY FARM

Makes 8 servings
Prep. Time: 20 minutes  Cooking time: 15 minutes

1 whole boneless chicken breast

half a red, *or* green, bell pepper, quartered

5 whole asparagus spears

1 small zucchini, quartered lengthwise

1 Tbsp. olive oil

½ cup onions, chopped

½ cup fresh mushrooms, sliced

2 garlic cloves, minced

2 heads romaine lettuce, chopped

¼-lb. (approx.) spring greens mix

1 cup shredded cheese

sunflower seeds, *optional*

soybeans, *optional*

craisins, *optional*

croutons, *optional*

favorite salad dressing, *optional*

1. Grill chicken breast, pepper, asparagus, and zucchini until just cooked through.

2. Sauté onions, mushrooms, and garlic in olive oil in skillet, just until slightly softened.

3. When cool enough to handle, slice grilled chicken and chop grilled vegetables.

4. Arrange bed of lettuce on large serving platter.

5. Arrange chicken over lettuce.

6. Spoon grilled and sautéed vegetables, spring greens mix, and cheese over lettuce and chicken.

7. Add your choice of sunflower seeds, soybeans, craisins, or croutons.

8. Pass your favorite salad dressing with the salad.

TIP

I like to add whatever vegetables are in season to this very versatile salad.

Wheat Berry Tabbouleh

Christine Hess
WENDY JO'S HOMEMADE

Makes 6 servings ❧ *Prep. Time: 20 minutes*
Cooking Time: 1 hour ❧ *Soaking Time: 8 hours, or overnight* ❧ *Cooling Time: 1 hour*

1 cup dry wheat berries

2 cups water, *or* vegetable broth

¾ cup chopped tomatoes

¾ cup chopped cucumber

½ cup chopped fresh parsley

¼ cup thinly sliced green onions

1 Tbsp. fresh mint, *or* 1 tsp. dried mint

3 Tbsp. extra-virgin olive oil

3 Tbsp. lemon juice

½ tsp. kosher salt

sliced cucumber, *optional*

sliced lemon, *optional*

TIPS

1. *You can make the salad ahead and chill it for up to 24 hours before serving.*

2. *Just before serving, arrange cucumber and lemon slices around edge of serving bowl, if you wish.*

1. Place dry wheat berries in good-sized stockpot. Pour in water, enough to rise 1" above the submerged berries. Soak for 8 hours or overnight.

2. Drain. Return soaked wheat berries to stockpot. Add water or broth. Partially cover and bring to a boil. Simmer, partially covered, for 1 hour, or until tender. (This should result in 2⅔ cups cooked wheat berries.)

3. Set cooked wheat berries aside to cool to room temperature.

4. Drain berries. Mix in large bowl with tomatoes, chopped cucumber, parsley, green onions, and mint.

5. Combine oil, lemon juice, and salt in jar with tight-fitting lid. Cover and shake well.

6. Slowly pour dressing over wheat berry mixture. Toss to coat.

Chicken Curry Grape Salad

Sue Eshleman
CENTRAL MARKET CUSTOMER

Makes 4 servings

Cooking Time: 10 minutes ❦ *Prep. Time: 45 minutes*

1 lb. boneless, skinless chicken breast pieces

salt to taste

2 cups red grapes, halved lengthwise

½ cup mayonnaise

2 tsp. curry powder

2 Tbsp. lemon juice

3 Tbsp. fresh parsley, finely chopped

½ tsp. salt

½ cup toasted almonds, sliced

1. Cook chicken with just a bit of salt.

2. Cut chicken into bite-sized pieces or shred with fingers. Place in mixing bowl.

3. Gently stir in grapes. Chill until needed.

4. In a separate bowl, blend together mayonnaise, curry powder, lemon juice, parsley, and ½ tsp. salt.

5. Stir dressing into chicken and grapes.

6. Just before serving, sprinkle with almonds.

TIPS

1. *Sometimes I use 2 6-oz. cans albacore tuna, drained, instead of chicken.*

2. *This is a versatile recipe, good in a pita pocket, or as a salad for a summer meal served on a bed of greens.*

Celery, Crab and Chicken Salad

Trish Hillegas

SWEETHEARTS OF LANCASTER COUNTY

Makes 3 servings ❧ *Prep. Time: 15 minutes*

lettuce leaves

1 cup chopped celery

1 cup crabmeat

1 cup chopped, cooked chicken

¼–½ cup chopped onion, depending on your taste preference

3 Tbsp. fresh parsley

¼ cup, or more, Russian dressing

whole ripe tomato

1. Place bed of lettuce leaves on each salad or small dinner plate.

2. In a medium-sized bowl, mix celery, crab, chicken, onion, and parsley with Russian dressing.

3. Place mixture on top lettuce bed on each plate.

4. Cut tomato into wedges. Garnish each plate with a wedge or two.

5. Serve immediately.

Deviled Eggs

Anna Marie Groff

ANNA MARIE GROFF'S FLOWERS

Makes 8-10 servings
Prep. Time: 15 minutes ❧ *Cooking Time: 8 minutes*

8 hard-boiled eggs

4 tsp. vinegar

2 Tbsp. mayonnaise

4 tsp. sugar

¼ tsp. salt

⅛–¼ tsp. pepper, according to your taste preferences

fresh parsley leaves

1. Cut eggs in half length-wise.

2. Remove yolks. Place in medium-sized bowl. Mash yolks with fork.

3. Add vinegar, mayonnaise, sugar, salt, and pepper to yolks.

4. Mix well with fork.

5. Spoon yolk mixture back into empty cooked egg whites.

6. Garnish with parsley flakes.

Celery Seed Dressing

Joanne Warfel
S. CLYDE WEAVER, INC.

Makes about 2½ cups dressing
Prep. Time: 10 minutes

1 small onion, diced
1 tsp. salt
1 tsp. dry mustard
1 tsp. celery seed
1 tsp. paprika
½ cup vinegar
1 cup sugar
1 cup cooking oil

1. Put all ingredients except cooking oil in blender.
2. Blend thoroughly.
3. Add cooking oil.
4. Blend again.
5. Refrigerate until ready to use over lettuce salads. Stir thoroughly just before using.

Pennsylvania Dutch Dressing

Arlene Leaman
S. CLYDE WEAVER, INC.

Makes 2 cups
Prep. Time: 10 minutes

½ cup oil
⅓ cup vinegar of your choice
¾ cup sugar
1 tsp. salt
1 tsp. dry mustard
1 tsp. celery seed
½ cup mayonnaise

1. Mix all ingredients together in blender.
2. Pour into an air-tight container and store in refrigerator.

TIP

Mix this dressing with shredded cabbage and you'll have a wonderful cole slaw. Or use it with a garden salad that is full of fresh vegetables.

Honey Poppy Seed Dressing

Ethel Stoner
STONER'S VEGETABLES

Makes 1 cup
Prep. Time: 10 minutes

Dressing:
1 green onion, minced
½ cup vegetable oil
½ cup honey
2 Tbsp. rice vinegar
1 tsp. poppy seeds
1 Tbsp. prepared mustard
½ tsp. celery seed
¼ tsp. salt

Salad:
arugula *or* salad greens of your choice
2 ozs. feta cheese
your favorite nuts
fruit in season

1. Combine onion, oil, honey, vinegar, poppy seeds, mustard, celery seed, and salt in a jar with a tight-fitting lid. Keep cool until ready to use.

2. Shake well and then drizzle over arugula or salad greens with crumbled feta cheese tossed in.

3. Or combine with your favorite nuts (I like cashews or almonds) and seasonal fresh fruit, for example, strawberries, pears, peaches, and berries.

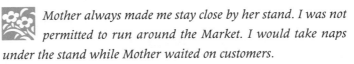

Mother always made me stay close by her stand. I was not permitted to run around the Market. I would take naps under the stand while Mother waited on customers.

— VIV HUNT, Viv's Varieties

SOUPS

Country French Vegetable Soup

Christine Hess
WENDY JO'S HOMEMADE

Makes 8-10 servings
Prep. Time: 30 minutes ❦ Cooking Time: 35 minutes

2 tsp. olive oil
2 cups chopped green cabbage
1 cup chopped onions
1 cup chopped carrots
1 cup sliced celery
1 cup diced red-skinned potatoes
1 tsp. caraway seeds
1 cup water
4 cups, *or* 2 14½-oz. cans, vegetable broth
1 cup drained chickpeas (garbanzo beans)
2 Tbsp. minced fresh parsley
2 tsp. chopped fresh dill, *or* ½ tsp. dried dill
½ tsp. black pepper

1. Heat oil until hot in large soup pot over medium-high heat.

2. Add cabbage, onions, carrots, celery, potatoes, and caraway seeds. Sauté two minutes.

3. Add water and broth. Bring to boil.

4. Reduce heat and simmer, covered, 30 minutes.

5. Add chickpeas, parsley, dill, and pepper.

6. Cook, covered, until thoroughly heated, about 5 minutes.

Hearty Potato Soup

Carl Charles

S. CLYDE WEAVER, INC.

Makes 4–5 servings

Prep. Time: 20 minutes   Cooking Time: 20 minutes

6–8 medium-sized red-skinned potatoes, unpeeled

1 cup water

1 tsp. parsley, chopped

½ tsp. salt

¼ tsp. onion powder

⅛ tsp. pepper

¼ tsp. celery seed

1 pint light cream

1–2 Tbsp. instant potato flakes

1–2 cups milk

6–8 hard-boiled eggs, shelled

2 cups shredded cheddar cheese

4–6 slices smoked bacon, cooked and chopped

1. Dice and boil potatoes in 1 cup water in soup pot until tender. Drain off most of the water.

2. Add parsley, salt, onion powder, pepper, celery seed, and light cream.

3. Smash the potatoes *slightly* with a potato masher.

4. Add potato flakes to thicken.

5. Add milk to make a soup consistency. Heat until warm.

6. Dice eggs into soup bowls and ladle soup on top.

7. Top individual servings with cheese and bacon.

NOTE

This is one of our favorite recipes for chilly winter nights. With the toppings, it is almost a stew.

Wilde Soupe

Barbara Zink
THE HERB SHOP

Makes: 10 servings
Prep. Time: 12 minutes ❧ *Cooking Time: 1¾ hours*

½ oz. dried wild mushroom pieces

1 cup boiling water

2 Tbsp. olive oil

2 Tbsp. butter

½ oz. wild mushroom powder

1 rounded Tbsp. dried minced onion

½ tsp. dried thyme

½ tsp. celery seed

2 Tbsp. flour

8 cups chicken stock

8 ozs. uncooked basmati and wild rice, mixed

1 bay leaf

½ cup light cream

2 Tbsp. bourbon, *optional*

fresh parsley, minced

1. Place dried mushrooms in a small bowl and break up any large pieces.

2. Cover with boiling water. Soak for 10 minutes.

3. In a large soup kettle, heat olive oil and butter over medium high heat. Add seasonings and stir for 1 minute.

4. Sprinkle with flour and stir about 1 minute, until well blended.

5. Add the soaked mushrooms and their liquid. Stir constantly until thickened.

6. Add chicken stock, dry rice, and bay leaf. Bring to a boil. Cover with lid slightly ajar. Lower heat and simmer for 1½ hours.

7. Add light cream and bourbon. Simmer 5 minutes.

8. Garnish with fresh parsley. Serve with leafy green salad and a crusty baguette.

Butternut Squash Soup from Scratch
with a baby-food bonus

Leah Margeriem
THIS LITTLE PIGGY

Makes 6-8 servings
Prep. Time: 30 minutes ❦ *Cooking Time: 1 hour*

3–4 butternut squash
1–2 Tbsp. olive oil
salt to taste
½ cup diced onions
2 carrots, diced
2 ribs celery, diced
2–3 Tbsp. butter
4–5 cups chicken, *or* vegetable, stock
1 cup heavy cream, *or* half and half
salt and pepper
cinnamon

1. Heat oven to 400°.

2. Halve squash lengthwise and scoop out seeds.

3. Clean flesh from seeds and toss with olive oil. Spread on baking sheet and sprinkle with salt. Place in oven to brown.

4. Place squash, cut side down, in glass baking dish. Roast squash in oven until skin pierces easily and begins to brown, about 1 hour. (Seeds and squash can be done at same time.)

5. Meanwhile, sauté onions, carrots, and celery in butter in skillet until soft.

6. When squash is soft, scoop flesh from skins and purée in blender or food processor.

7. Add sautéed veggies and some of the stock, blending until smooth.

8. Pour into stockpot. Add cream. Add more stock until of desired consistency.

9. Add salt and pepper to taste.

10. Serve warm, garnished with squash seeds and cinnamon.

TIPS

1. *Reserve some roasted squash for puréeing with water, formula, or breast milk for a perfect first baby food.*

2. *Freeze squash purée in ice cube trays for future feedings.*

Convenient Pumpkin/Squash Soup

Ruth Thomas
THOMAS PRODUCE

Makes 4-6 servings
Prep. Time: 10-20 minutes ❦ Cooking Time: 15 minutes

⅓ cup onion, chopped

3 Tbsp. butter

3 Tbsp. flour

½–1 tsp. salt, according to your taste preference

½ tsp. nutmeg

½ tsp. ginger, *or* curry powder

2 cups chicken broth

2 cups cooked squash, mashed, *or* canned pumpkin

2 cups heavy cream

1. In a good-sized saucepan, sauté onion in butter until transparent.

2. In a separate small bowl, combine flour, salt, nutmeg, and ginger or curry powder.

3. Add to onion mixture to make a paste.

4. Add chicken broth and mashed squash. Stir until combined.

5. Add heavy cream. Simmer, partially covered, until thoroughly heated. Do not boil.

6. Serve immediately.

TESTER TIPS

1. *For a lower-calorie dish, substitute 1½ cups 2% milk and ½ cup evaporated milk for 2 cups heavy cream.*

2. *Top each individual serving with a dollop of sour cream and a sprinkle of chopped chives.*

NOTE

As the warm summer days fade and cooler weather comes and frost appears on the pumpkins, I am bombarded with requests for cooked, mashed squash that I prepare for eager customers. I get the most requests for this ingredient and this recipe.

Russian Cabbage Borscht

Janelle and Kendal Yoder

LETTUCE TOSS SALAD

Makes 6–8 servings, or 2½ quarts
Prep. Time: 30 minutes ❧ Cooking Time: 1–1¼ hours

1½ cups thinly sliced potatoes
1 cup thinly sliced beets
4 cups vegetable stock, *or* water
1½ cups chopped onions
2 Tbsp. butter
1 scant tsp. caraway seeds
2 tsp. salt
1 rib celery, chopped
1 large carrot, sliced
3 cups chopped cabbage
1 Tbsp. raisins
black pepper
¼ tsp. dillweed
1 Tbsp. plus 1 tsp. cider vinegar
1 Tbsp. plus 1 tsp. honey
1 cup tomato purée

Toppings:
sour cream
dillweed
chopped fresh tomato

1. Place potatoes, beets, and stock in medium-sized saucepan and cook until vegetables are tender. Drain, reserving cooking stock.

2. In large soup kettle, begin cooking onions in butter. Add caraway seeds and salt. Cook until onion is translucent.

3. Add celery, carrots, and cabbage. Add reserved cooking water from beets and potatoes. Cook, covered, until all vegetables are tender.

4. Add cooked potatoes and beets, raisins, black pepper, dillweed, vinegar, honey, and tomato purée to soup kettle.

5. Cover and simmer slowly for at least 30 minutes. Taste to correct seasonings.

6. Serve topped with sour cream, extra dillweed, and chopped fresh tomatoes.

TIP

Thirty minutes is definitely the minimum for simmering the borscht. When I have the time I let it simmer for an hour or longer. This makes the raisins puff up. They almost look like grapes again. Yummy! You can thin the soup with water at the end of the cooking time.

Cream of Asparagus Soup

Ethel Stoner

STONER'S VEGETABLES

Makes 4-6 servings
Prep. Time: 15 minutes ❧ Cooking Time: 20 minutes

1 lb. fresh asparagus

3 Tbsp. butter

1 small onion, diced

3 cups chicken stock

1 small potato, diced

8-oz. pkg. cream cheese, softened, *divided*

1 tsp. pepper

1 tsp. chives

½ cup Parmesan cheese

1. Cut asparagus into 1"-long pieces.

2. In a good-sized saucepan, melt butter. Add onion and sauté until tender but not browned.

3. Add chicken stock, cut-up asparagus, and diced potato. Cook till potatoes are fork-tender.

4. Purée half the broth and vegetables with half the cream cheese in blender.

5. Repeat with remaining broth, vegetables, and cheese.

6. Return puréed mixture to cooking pot. Add seasonings and cheese.

7. Serve hot.

Chilled Cucumber Soup

Janelle Glick
LANCASTER GENERAL WELLNESS PARTNERSHIP

Makes 4-5 servings
Prep. Time: 10 minutes ❧ *Chilling Time: 2 hours*

1 very large seedless cucumber

1 pint plain, low-fat yogurt

1–4 garlic cloves, crushed and minced, amount depending upon your taste preference

3 Tbsp. walnut pieces

1 medium-sized bunch fresh dill

1. Peel and cut cucumber into ½"-thick slices.

2. Place in blender in this order: cucumber slices, yogurt, minced garlic, nuts, and dill. Purée.

3. Chill 2 hours before serving.

Celery Soup

Trish Hillegas
SWEETHEARTS OF LANCASTER COUNTY

Makes 3-4 servings
Prep. Time: 20 minutes ❧ *Cooking Time: 20 minutes*

3 Tbsp. butter

14-oz. can chicken broth

2 good-sized ribs of celery

1 small onion

2 cups boiling water

1 Tbsp. flour

2 cups milk, *divided*

1 stem fresh parsley leaves, chopped

½ tsp. salt

dash of pepper

1. Place butter and chicken broth in medium-sized saucepan.

2. Chop celery and onion in small pieces.

3. Add vegetables to saucepan. Simmer, partially covered, for five minutes.

4. Add water and cook till celery and onion are soft.

5. Meanwhile, shake flour and 1 cup milk together in covered jar until smooth.

6. Gradually stir into broth. Then add remaining milk, stirring till smooth.

7. Add parsley. Cook 5 minutes.

8. Season and serve.

Fresh Berry Soup

Janelle and Kendal Yoder
LETTUCE TOSS SALAD

Makes 4-6 servings
Prep. Time: 15 minutes ❦ *Chilling Time: 1-2 hours*

1 quart fresh orange juice

4 cups plain yogurt, *or* buttermilk, *or* sour cream, *or* a combination of all three

1 Tbsp. honey

2 Tbsp. fresh lemon, *or* lime, juice

1½ pints fresh raspberries, *or* blueberries, *or* strawberries, *or* some combination of them

dash of cinnamon

dash of nutmeg

fresh mint

1. In a large mixing bowl, whisk together first four ingredients.

2. Wash and drain berries. (Leave smaller berries whole, but slice strawberries.)

3. Gently stir berries into soup base.

4. Fold in cinnamon and nutmeg.

5. Chill thoroughly.

6. Garnish individual servings with a sprig of mint.

TIP

When I don't have fresh berries on hand, I use frozen ones. I chop them lightly in a blender or food processor before stirring them into the soup.

White Chicken Chili

Becky Friedrich
THOMAS PRODUCE

Makes 4-6 servings
Prep. Time: 40 minutes ❦ Cooking Time: 15 minutes

½ cup onion, chopped
½ cup green bell pepper, chopped
3 ribs celery, chopped
¼ cup mild green chilies
1 clove garlic, minced
1 Tbsp. vegetable oil
2 Tbsp. butter
2 Tbsp. flour
2 cups chicken broth
½ cup milk
2 cups white kidney beans, *or* 15½-oz. can, drained
2 cups corn, fresh, *or* frozen, *or* canned
2 cups cooked chicken
¼ cup sour cream
1 tsp. poultry seasoning
1 tsp. cumin
salt to taste
pepper to taste
cheddar cheese, shredded

1. In a large skillet sauté onion, bell pepper, celery, chilies, and garlic in oil.

2. Set aside.

3. Melt butter in a good-sized saucepan. Blend in flour. Cook until bubbly.

4. Stir in broth and milk. Cook over medium heat, stirring until sauce thickens and is smooth.

5. Add beans, corn, chicken, sour cream, poultry seasoning, and cumin.

6. Add sautéed vegetables.

7. Season to taste with salt and pepper.

8. Sprinkle each individual serving with cheddar cheese.

Chicken Tortilla Soup

Janelle and Kendal Yoder
LETTUCE TOSS SALAD

Makes 15-20 servings, or 5 quarts
Prep. Time: 20-25 minutes ❦ *Cooking Time: 30 minutes*

4 ribs celery, chopped

2 Tbsp. olive oil, *divided*

1 large onion, chopped

half a green bell pepper, chopped

3 chicken breast halves, cubed

lemon pepper to taste

2 48-oz. cans chicken broth

2 14-oz. cans black beans, drained

2 14-oz. cans pinto beans, drained

2 pints frozen corn

16-oz. jar medium salsa

garlic salt to taste

onion powder to taste

dried oregano to taste

salt to taste

Toppings:

tortilla chips, crushed

cheddar *or* Mexican-blend
shredded cheese

sour cream

1. Sauté celery in 1 Tbsp. oil in soup pot until partially softened. Stir in onion and bell pepper. Continue sautéing until vegetables are tender.

2. Brown cubed chicken breast in 1 Tbsp. oil in skillet. Season with lemon pepper.

3. Add seasoned chicken to soup pot, along with any drippings or broth from cooking the chicken.

4. Add canned chicken broth, beans, corn, salsa, and seasonings.

5. Cook until corn is tender.

6. Serve in bowls topped with tortilla chips, cheese, and sour cream.

NOTE

This recipe was passed on to me from my husband's aunt when we got married. It's a favorite of her family, and now ours as well.

Beef Barley Soup

Joanne Warfel
S. CLYDE WEAVER, INC.

Makes 8-10 servings
Prep. Time: 1 hour ❧ *Cooking Time: 1½–1¾ hours*

1 lb. ground beef
1 quart water
1 quart tomato juice
2 beef bouillon cubes
¼–½ cup medium pearl barley, uncooked
1½ cups diced carrots
1 small onion, chopped
1–2 medium potatoes, diced
2 tsp. garlic salt
1 tsp. onion powder
2 tsp. dried parsley
1 tsp. pepper
¼–½ tsp. salt, according to your taste preference

1. Brown beef in a large soup pot. Drain off drippings.

2. Add water, tomato juice, bouillon cubes, and barley to beef.

3. Cover and simmer 1 hour.

4. Add remaining ingredients.

5. Cover and simmer until vegetables are tender, about 30–45 more minutes.

Sweet Potato and Andouille Soup

Michael L. Ervin
CENTRAL MARKET MANAGER

Makes 8 servings
Prep. Time: 20 minutes ❧ *Cooking Time: 1 hour*

¼ lb. andouille turkey sausage, diced

half a stick (4 Tbsp.) unsalted butter, *divided*

1¼ cups onions, finely chopped

1 tsp. dried thyme, crumbled

1½ lbs. sweet potatoes, peeled and cut into ½" cubes

7 cups chicken broth

¼ cup brown sugar, packed

¼ cup plus 2 Tbsp. heavy cream

salt to taste

pepper to taste

nutmeg, *or* cinnamon, to taste

1. In a large soup kettle, cook turkey sausage in 2 Tbsp. butter over moderate heat for 5 minutes.

2. Add onions. Cook until onions are soft.

3. Add thyme and sweet potatoes. Cook while stirring for 5 minutes.

4. Stir in broth and brown sugar.

5. Simmer, partially covered, over moderately-low heat for 45 minutes, or until sweet potatoes are tender.

6. In a blender or food processor, purée soup in batches, transferring it when puréed into a good-sized saucepan.

7. Stir in cream and remaining 2 Tbsp. butter.

8. Add salt and pepper to taste.

9. Garnish with a dash of nutmeg or cinnamon just before serving.

I first tasted this soup at some Market friends' home. The guests included a group of regular Market shoppers who were together for dinner and conversation.

— MICHAEL L. ERVIN, Central Market Manager

Heidi's Lentil Soup

Henner and Heidi Steinle
THE GERMAN DELI

Makes 6 servings
Prep. Time: 15 minutes ❧ Cooking Time: 1½–2 hours

1 lb. dry lentils

8–10 cups water

1 medium onion

10 whole cloves

6 bay leaves

4 beef bouillon cubes

1–2 Tbsp. Vegeta, *or your favorite seasoning blend*

1 Tbsp. onion powder

1 Tbsp. seasoning salt

¼ tsp. nutmeg

2 smoked ham hocks

1-lb. pkg. baby carrots

white vinegar, *optional*

1. Rinse lentils and place in large stock pot.

2. Cover with 8–10 cups water.

3. Peel onion and leave whole. Press cloves into onion. Add onion to pot.

4. Add bay leaves, bouillon cubes, various seasonings, ham hocks, and carrots.

5. Cover and bring to a boil.

6. Reduce heat and simmer, partially covered, until lentils and ham hocks are soft, from 1½–2 hours.

7. When finished cooking, discard onion and bay leaves.

8. Debone ham. Cut meat into bite-sized pieces. Return to soup.

9. Finish with a dash of white vinegar, if you wish, just before serving.

VEGETABLES

Roasted Asparagus

Karen Paul
S. CLYDE WEAVER, INC.

Makes 6-8 servings
Prep. Time: 15 minutes ❧ *Baking Time: 12 minutes*

2 lbs. asparagus, bottom ends trimmed

2–3 Tbsp. olive oil, *or* cooking spray

¼ tsp. kosher salt

⅛ tsp. cracked pepper

2 Tbsp. butter

2 tsp. soy sauce

1 tsp. balsamic vinegar

1. Preheat oven to 400°.

2. Arrange asparagus in single layer on lightly greased baking sheet.

3. Drizzle with olive oil, tossing to coat, or spray with cooking spray. Sprinkle with salt and pepper.

4. Bake 12 minutes, or until just tender.

5. Melt butter in pan over medium heat for approximately 3 minutes, or until nutty brown.

6. Remove from heat. Stir in soy sauce and balsamic vinegar.

7. Drizzle over asparagus, tossing to coat.

8. Serve immediately.

Asparagus with Toasted Almonds

Linda Rittenhouse
TURKEY LADY

Makes 6 servings
Prep. Time: 15 minutes ❦ *Cooking Time: 13–15 minutes*

2 lbs. fresh asparagus

Dressing:

half a stick (4 Tbsp.) unsalted butter

¼ cup olive oil

¾ cup toasted slivered almonds,
or pine nuts

⅓ cup balsamic vinegar

salt

freshly ground pepper

1. Trim asparagus spears to the same length.

2. Bring about 2 inches salted water to boil in a large sauté pan.

3. Lay asparagus in pan and cook, uncovered, until tender-crisp, about 3–5 minutes.

4. Remove asparagus and plunge into cold water.

5. Drain and pat dry.

6. To prepare Dressing, heat butter and oil in a large sauté pan.

7. Add nuts and stir until hot.

8. Add vinegar and heat. When bubbly, pour over prepared asparagus.

9. Salt and pepper to taste.

10. Serve hot, or cooled to room temperature.

Party Carrots

Doris Kiefer
KIEFER MEATS

Makes 4-6 servings
Prep. Time: 30 minutes ❧ Baking Time: 30 minutes

3 cups carrots, sliced

4 strips bacon, cooked and crumbled

1 tsp. minced onion

½ tsp. salt

¼ tsp. pepper

3 Tbsp. brown sugar

3 Tbsp. melted butter

1. Cook carrots until just tender.

2. Place carrots in a greased 1-quart baking dish.

3. Stir in bacon, minced onion, salt, and pepper.

4. Sprinkle with brown sugar.

5. Top with melted butter.

6. Bake, covered, at 400° for 30 minutes.

Roasted Cauliflower

Ruth Thomas
THOMAS PRODUCE

Makes 4-6 servings
Prep. Time: 10 minutes ❧ Marinating Time: 15-20 minutes ❧ Roasting Time: 20 minutes

1 small head cauliflower

¼ cup vegetable, *or* olive, oil

1 tsp. salt

½ tsp. black pepper

1 tsp. chili powder

1 tsp. onion powder

¼ tsp. dried oregano

VARIATION

You can exchange parsnips, sweet potatoes, red beets, or any root vegetable for the cauliflower.

1. Wash cauliflower and break into small florets. Pat dry.

2. Mix oil and seasonings in a bowl.

3. Place cauliflower in a zip-closure bag. Add seasoned oil to bag.

4. Marinate 15-20 minutes, flipping occasionally.

5. Place cauliflower and oil in a lightly greased baking pan in a single layer.

6. Roast, uncovered, at 450° for 20 minutes. Stir occasionally so that the vegetable cooks evenly.

Orange Beets

Ethel Stoner
STONER'S VEGETABLES

Makes 4 servings
Prep. Time: 15 minutes ❧ Cooking Time: 20–25 minutes

2–3 medium-sized beets, peeled and grated
½ cup onion, chopped
2 Tbsp. butter
1 Tbsp. flour
3 Tbsp. orange juice
1 Tbsp. vinegar
3 Tbsp. brown sugar
¼ tsp. nutmeg

1. Cook grated beets in small amount of salt water until crispy tender, about 10–12 minutes. Drain. Set aside and keep warm.

2. In a small saucepan, sauté onion in butter. Stir in flour, orange juice, vinegar, and sugar. Cook, stirring constantly, until thickened and well blended.

3. Pour sauce over cooked beets. Season with nutmeg and serve.

Old-Fashioned Corn Fritters

Marian A Sweigart
S. CLYDE WEAVER, INC.

Makes 3–4 servings
Prep. Time: 10 minutes ❧ Cooking Time: 8–10 minutes per skillet-full

2 cups fresh corn, *or* frozen *or* canned, drained
2 eggs, beaten
¼ cup flour
1 tsp. baking powder
1 tsp. salt
⅛ tsp. pepper
2 Tbsp. cream
4 Tbsp. shortening, *divided*

1. Combine corn, beaten eggs, flour, baking powder, salt, and pepper in a good-sized mixing bowl.

2. Mix thoroughly, and then stir in cream.

3. Melt half the shortening in skillet. Carefully drop corn mixture by ¼ cupfuls into hot shortening. Allow plenty of space around each fritter so they brown rather than steam.

4. When fritters have browned on one side (about 3–4 minutes), flip carefully and brown on other side.

5. Remove fully browned fritters to plate and keep warm.

6. Repeat with remaining corn mixture.

7. Serve immediately.

Country-Style Escalloped Corn

Pamela Brenner
LANCASTER JUICE CO.

Makes 6 servings
Prep. Time: 15–20 minutes ❧ *Baking Time: 60–65 minutes*

1 Tbsp. butter

1 large yellow onion

1 rib celery, finely chopped

1 large egg, slightly beaten

1 large egg white

¾ cup crushed low-sodium crackers, *divided*

¾ cup milk

2 Tbsp. chopped, drained, canned pimientos, *optional*

1 tsp. dry mustard

¼–½ tsp. salt, according to your taste preference

⅛ tsp. cayenne pepper

3 cups fresh corn

3 cups creamed corn

1 Tbsp. butter, melted

1. Preheat oven to 350°.

2. In small saucepan over moderate heat, melt 1 Tbsp. butter. Add onion and celery and cook until tender, approximately 5 minutes.

3. In medium bowl, combine egg and egg white, ½ cup crackers, milk, pimentos if you wish, mustard, salt, and pepper.

4. Stir in onion mixture and the corns.

5. Pour into a lightly greased 1½-quart casserole.

6. In small bowl, stir together remaining ¼ cup crackers and 1 Tbsp. melted butter. Sprinkle over corn mixture.

7. Bake, uncovered, approximately 1 hour, or until knife comes out clean when inserted in center.

TIP

I usually double this recipe and bake it in a large casserole dish.

Fresh Corn and Zucchini Medley

Dawn Meck
MECK'S PRODUCE

Makes 4-6 servings
Prep. Time: 10-15 minutes ❦ Cooking Time: 15 minutes

4 slices bacon

2 cups unpeeled zucchini, chopped coarsely

1½ cups fresh corn kernels

1 small onion, chopped

dash of pepper

½ cup shredded cheddar cheese

1. Sauté bacon slices in skillet until evenly browned and crispy.

2. Remove bacon and cool. Drain drippings, reserving 1 Tbsp. drippings in skillet.

3. Sauté zucchini, corn, and onion in drippings until tender, about 10 minutes.

4. Crumble bacon. Toss with sautéed vegetables.

5. Sprinkle with pepper just before serving.

6. Top with shredded cheese and serve.

NOTE

This is a favorite summer dish for our family. It is a wonderful complement to any grilled main course.

The mother of Charles Demuth used to shop at Central Market. Many of the beautiful fruits and vegetables which appear in his paintings were purchased from the produce stands of Lancaster County farmers.

— GERALDINE ALVAREZ

Creamy Zucchini Bake

Deb Becker

CENTRAL MARKET CUSTOMER

Makes 6–8 servings
Prep. Time: 25 minutes   Baking Time: 25 minutes

3 zucchini, approximately 1½ lbs.
1 large carrot, grated
1 onion, chopped
6-oz. box stuffing mix
1 stick (8 Tbsp.) butter

Sauce:
10¾-oz. can cream of mushroom soup
½ cup sour cream
½ cup shredded cheddar cheese

1. Chop zucchini into 1" chunks.

2. Place in saucepan along with grated carrot and chopped onion. Steam for a few minutes, until vegetables are just tender. Drain well.

3. While vegetables are steaming, mix Sauce ingredients in another saucepan. Stir frequently to mix well. Heat until cheese melts and Sauce is smooth.

4. Fold steamed vegetables into sauce.

5. Melt butter.

6. Place bread crumbs in mixing bowl. Stir in melted butter.

7. Layer half of bread crumbs onto bottom of greased 9" × 13" baking pan.

8. Spoon zucchini-sauce mixture evenly over crumbs.

9. Sprinkle with rest of bread crumbs.

10. Bake, uncovered, at 350° for 25 minutes.

South of the Border Squash

Pamela Brenner
LANCASTER JUICE CO.

Makes 6 servings
Prep. Time: 20–30 minutes ❧ Baking Time: 25–30 minutes

1½ lbs. summer squash, zucchini
or yellow

1 medium onion, chopped

2 Tbsp. butter

4-oz. can chopped chilies

2 Tbsp. flour

1 tsp. salt

¼–½ tsp. pepper, according to
your taste preference

1½ cups grated Monterey Jack
cheese

1 egg

1 cup cottage cheese

2 Tbsp. parsley

½ cup grated Parmesan cheese

1. Dice squash. Sauté in good-sized skillet with onion in butter until tender-crisp.

2. Fold in chilies, flour, salt, and pepper.

3. Place in greased 2-quart baking dish. Sprinkle with Monterey Jack cheese.

4. In a bowl, combine egg, cottage cheese, and parsley. Spread over cheese.

5. Sprinkle with Parmesan cheese.

6. Bake uncovered at 400° for 25–30 minutes, or until heated through.

NOTE

This is a good accompaniment to chicken or burgers from the grill.

VARIATION

I use tapioca flour to make this gluten-free. I also use hot peppers from the garden instead of the chilies to make it hotter. If you like it spicier yet, use hot cheese instead of the Monterey Jack.

Mixed Greens and Cabbage

Janelle Glick

LANCASTER GENERAL WELLNESS PARTNERSHIP

Makes 6 servings

Prep. Time: 20 minutes ❧ *Cooking Time: 1 hour*

1 tsp. olive oil

half a medium onion, thinly sliced

2 cups fat-free, low-sodium chicken broth

2 Tbsp. imitation bacon bits

1 tsp. garlic powder

1 tsp. celery seeds

¼ tsp. pepper

pinch–¼ tsp. crushed red pepper flakes, depending upon your tolerance for spiciness and heat

¼ lb. fresh collard greens

¼ lb. fresh kale

½ lb. green cabbage

1. In large saucepan, heat oil over medium heat, swirling to coat bottom.

2. Add onion and cook 2–3 minutes, or until tender-crisp, stirring occasionally.

3. Stir in broth, bacon bits, garlic powder, celery seeds, pepper, and red pepper flakes.

4. Increase heat to medium-high and bring to a simmer. Reduce heat and continue simmering, covered, for 4–5 minutes so flavors blend.

5. Meanwhile, trim stems from collard greens and kale. Discard stems.

6. Core cabbage. Discard core.

7. Coarsely chop greens and cabbage and stir into simmering broth mixture.

8. Increase heat to medium-high until mixture returns to a simmer.

9. Reduce heat and simmer, covered, 35–45 minutes, or until greens and cabbage are tender, stirring occasionally.

10. Ladle greens and cooking liquid into bowls and serve.

Red Cabbage and Apples

Sam Neff

S. CLYDE WEAVER, INC.

Makes: 20 servings
Prep. Time: 40 minutes ❧ Cooking Time: 20–30 minutes

6 lbs. red cabbage, shredded

2 lbs. onions, sliced

6 tart Granny Smith apples,
sliced and peeled

3 Tbsp. butter

1 cup red wine vinegar

salt to taste

pepper to taste

1–2 tsp. sugar, *optional*

1. In large stockpot, sauté cabbage, onions, and apples in butter.

2. When cabbage is wilted, add vinegar and simmer until most of the liquid is evaporated. Add salt, pepper, and sugar.

3. Serve hot or cold. A good accompaniment to grilled meats and/or bratwurst, bockwurst, or German wieners.

Brussels Sprouts Sauté

FUNK BROTHERS, INC.

Makes 4 servings
Prep. Time: 10–15 minutes ❧ Cooking Time: 10–12 minutes

3 Tbsp. butter

2 large carrots, sliced

2 cups Brussels sprouts, halved

1 medium leek, sliced

1 Tbsp. water

¼ tsp. caraway seeds

¼ tsp. salt

¼ tsp. pepper

sour cream, *optional*

1. Melt butter in a large skillet over medium heat. Sauté carrots 3 minutes.

2. Stir in Brussels sprouts and sliced leek and sauté 2 more minutes.

3. Add water. Cover and steam 5 minutes, or until Brussels sprouts are crisp and tender. Add additional water if necessary.

4. Sprinkle with caraway seeds, salt, and pepper.

5. Serve with a dollop of sour cream on individual servings if you wish.

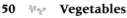

Spinach and Yogurt

Sam Neff
S. CLYDE WEAVER, INC.

Makes: 6 servings
Prep. Time: 15 minutes ❧ *Cooking Time: 15 minutes*

1 lb. fresh spinach, *or* 2 boxes frozen, thawed
1 medium onion, diced
1–2 garlic cloves, crushed
olive oil
½ tsp. turmeric
½–¾ tsp. cumin seeds, ground
¼ tsp. chili powder, mild *or* spicy
salt to taste
2 cups plain yogurt

1. Steam spinach. Drain.

2. Sauté onion and crushed garlic in olive oil in large skillet. Add spices. Brown slightly.

3. Add spinach. When spinach is hot, turn off heat. Add yogurt.

4. Slowly reheat if you wish, but watch carefully because cooked yogurt will separate.

NOTE

We enjoy serving this with roast leg of lamb, with a bit of lemon juice for the lamb and spinach. The dish can also be served cold or at room temperature.

Hot Herbed Tomatoes

Sam Neff
S. CLYDE WEAVER, INC.

Makes 6 servings
Prep. Time: 10 minutes ❦ Baking Time: 10 minutes ❦ Broiling Time: 6-8 minutes

2 pints cherry tomatoes
¾ cup bread crumbs
⅓ cup onion, minced
¼ cup fresh parsley, minced
1 clove garlic, minced
¾ tsp. salt
¼–½ tsp. thyme, according to your taste preference
¼ tsp. pepper
¼ cup olive oil

1. Place tomatoes in a single layer on baking sheet with sides. Bake at 375° for 10 minutes.

2. In a small bowl, mix all other ingredients together except olive oil.

3. Spoon over tomatoes. Drizzle olive oil over top.

4. Broil 6-8 minutes, or until browned and heated through. Serve immediately.

Baked Salsify Casserole

Ethel Stoner
STONER'S VEGETABLES

Makes 6 servings
Prep. Time: 20-30 minutes ❦ Baking Time: 45 minutes

2-4 salsify, enough to make 2 cups when cooked, *divided*
3 cups soda crackers, *divided*
salt and pepper
2 eggs
3 cups milk
2 Tbsp. butter

1. Clean salsify and cut into pieces.

2. Place in saucepan with water to steam. Cover and cook till just tender.

3. Crush crackers and scatter 1 cup over bottom of greased baking dish.

4. Layer half of cooked salsify over cracker crumbs. Sprinkle with salt and pepper.

5. Scatter another cup of crushed crackers over salsify.

6. Top with remaining salsify. Sprinkle with salt and pepper.

7. Cover with remaining crushed crackers.

8. In a mixing bowl, beat eggs and milk together. Pour over layered crackers and salsify.

9. Dot with butter.

10. Bake 45 minutes, uncovered, at 350°.

NOTE

Salsify is a vegetable that grows in cool weather. It's white and is shaped much like a carrot or parsnip. Its mild flavor has a hint of oyster. Many of our customers ask me for recipes for using the plant. This is one of my favorites.

Baked Lima Beans

Katie Stoltzfus
EISENBERGER'S BAKERY

Makes: 10–12 servings ❧ *Prep. Time: 30 minutes*
Soaking Time: 8 hours, or overnight ❧ *Cooking Time: 1½ hours* ❧ *Baking Time: 1½ hours*

1 lb. dried lima beans
½ lb. bacon
½ cup onion, minced
¾ cup celery, chopped
¾ cup sweet molasses
½ cup brown sugar
½ cup ketchup
1½ tsp. dry mustard
1½ tsp. salt
1½ cups cooking liquor *or* tomato juice
1½ Tbsp. Worcestershire sauce
⅛ tsp. pepper

1. Wash beans several times. Soak overnight, making sure they are well covered with water.

2. Cook beans in soaking water for about 1½ hours over low heat, adding more water if necessary. Do not allow beans to become too soft.

3. Sauté bacon until crisp. Drain on paper towels. Break bacon into small pieces. Reserve drippings.

4. Cook onions and celery in bacon drippings until onions become transparent.

5. Mix together all ingredients, saving some bacon for a garnish on top.

6. Bake, covered, at 350° for 1½ hours or more, until beans are tender.

Roasted Rosemary Sweet Potatoes

Sue Eshleman

Makes 4–5 servings
Prep. Time: 15 minutes Cooking Time: 20–25 minutes

4–5 sweet potatoes
3 Tbsp. olive oil
¾ tsp. garlic salt
1 tsp. crushed rosemary

1. Peel sweet potatoes and cut into short strips about 2" long and ½" thick. Place in mixing bowl.

2. Add olive oil to bowl with potatoes and stir well.

3. Sprinkle with garlic salt and rosemary. Stir well.

4. Spread on greased shallow baking pan with sides.

5. Bake at 400° for 20–25 minutes, or until fork-tender.

6. Stir or turn potatoes halfway through baking time.

TIP

Once when serving this to guests, I didn't have enough sweet potatoes, so I substituted with part white potatoes. The color combination was very attractive and quite delicious.

Red-Skinned Mashed Potatoes

Ruth Thomas
THOMAS PRODUCE

Makes 8-10 servings
Prep. Time: 10 minutes ❧ *Cooking Time: 20-30 minutes* ❧ *Baking Time: 30 minutes*

2½ lbs. red-skinned potatoes
1 clove garlic, minced
½ tsp. salt
½ cup sour cream
3-oz. pkg. cream cheese, softened
½ tsp. garlic salt
½ tsp. black pepper
half a stick (4 Tbsp.) butter, cut into chunks

1. Wash potatoes thoroughly. Do not peel. Cut into quarters.

2. Place potatoes, garlic, and ½ tsp. salt in soup pot. Add water to depth of 2".

3. Cover pot. Cook potatoes in water until soft, about 20-30 minutes.

4. Drain liquid.

5. Mash potatoes.

6. Add sour cream, cream cheese, garlic salt, pepper, and butter. Mix well.

7. Place in greased 2-quart baking dish.

8. Bake, uncovered, at 350° for 30 minutes.

Stalls outside, on the northern side of the Market House, are set apart for the sale of Fresh Fish, during market hours only; and it shall be unlawful to sell fresh fish anywhere else in the market limits.

The West King Street curb and the southwest angles of Centre Square are set apart for the sale of meat in not less quantities than by the quarter.

— MARKET RULES, 1889

Cheesy Au Gratin Potatoes

Sara Neilon
CENTRAL MARKET CUSTOMER

Makes 5-6 servings
Prep. Time: 20-30 minutes ❦ Cooking Time: 1 hour and 10 minutes

1¼ cups shredded sharp cheddar cheese

1¼ cup Lancaster Jack, *or* Monterey Jack, cheese

½ cup grated Parmesan cheese

2 tsp. cornstarch

3 lbs., *or* about 6 large, russet potatoes, sliced ⅛" thick, *divided*

1 tsp. salt, *divided*

½ tsp. pepper, *divided*

¾ cup heavy cream

½ cup low-sodium chicken broth

1. Grease a 2–3-quart gratin dish or very large pie plate.

2. Preheat oven to 350°.

3. Toss cheeses and cornstarch in bowl until well mixed.

4. Layer half of potatoes in dish in shingle-type pattern, circling around the dish.

5. Sprinkle evenly with 1½ cups cheese mixture, ½ tsp. salt, and ¼ tsp. ground pepper.

6. Layer remaining potatoes as before.

7. Sprinkle ¼ tsp. salt and ¼ tsp. pepper over top.

8. Combine cream and broth in small bowl. Pour over potatoes.

9. Top with remaining cheese mixture.

10. Cover with foil and bake until potatoes are nearly tender, about 55 minutes. Uncover and continue baking about 15 minutes, or until potatoes are tender and browned.

TIP

Use a mandolin slicer to make quick, uniform potato slices. Potatoes of even thickness are easier to layer in a "shingle" pattern in the plate.

Oven-Roasted Vegetables

Janelle Glick
LANCASTER GENERAL WELLNESS PARTNERSHIP

Makes 6 servings
Prep. Time: 15 minutes ❦ *Cooking Time: 40–45 minutes*

2 medium sweet potatoes, white potatoes, *or* 1 of each

1 cup baby carrots, *or* 2 regular carrots

1 medium parsnip, *optional*

1 red onion

1 Tbsp. olive oil

3 cloves garlic, minced

1 tsp. dried mixed herbs (for example, marjoram, thyme, rosemary, oregano) crushed

¼ tsp. salt

⅛ tsp. black pepper

1. Cut potatoes into 1" cubes. Place in large mixing bowl.

2. If using regular carrots, cut into 1" pieces. Add baby carrots, or carrot pieces, to potatoes in mixing bowl.

3. If using parsnip, cut into thin wedges. Add to vegetables in mixing bowl.

4. Cut red onion in thin wedges. Add to mixing bowl.

5. In small bowl, combine oil, garlic, mixed herbs, salt, and pepper.

6. Drizzle oil mixture over vegetables. Toss to coat.

7. Place prepared vegetables in lightly greased 9" × 13" baking dish. Cover with foil.

8. Bake in a 425° oven for 30 minutes.

9. Remove foil and stir vegetables.

10. Bake uncovered 5–10 minutes more, or until vegetables are tender.

Friday Night Baked Vegetables

Regine Ibold
REGINE'S COFFEE

Makes: 3-4 servings
Prep. Time: 20 minutes ❦ *Cooking Time: 35-45 minutes*

1½ lbs. red and green peppers, mixed

1 lb. new potatoes, unpeeled

1 large sweet onion

1 head garlic, flattened into cloves, unpeeled

¼ cup olive oil

coarse salt

freshly ground pepper

bunches of fresh thyme *or* rosemary

1. Cut peppers lengthwise into quarters. Remove seeds and membrane.

2. If potatoes are small, do not cut them. If larger, halve or quarter them.

3. Cut onion into eighths.

4. Place vegetables and garlic in large, shallow roasting pan. Toss well with olive oil, salt, pepper, and herbs.

5. Bake at 425° for 35 minutes, or until tender, tossing and shaking every 10 minutes.

6. Serve with French bread. Squeeze garlic out of skin onto each slice.

VARIATIONS

1. *Add halved plum tomatoes in Step 4.*

2. *Add blanched, sautéed sausage pieces in Step 5.*

3. *Add partially cooked chicken pieces in Step 5.*

4. *Add grated mozzarella at the end of baking, and allow cheese to melt.*

Vegetable Couscous

Ruth Thomas
THOMAS PRODUCE

Makes 4 servings
Prep. Time: 30 minutes ❧ Cooking Time: 15 minutes

1½ cup chicken broth, *or* vegetable broth

3 Tbsp. olive oil, *divided*

¾ tsp. salt

1 cup uncooked couscous

½ cup carrots, diced

½ cup onions, diced

½ cup bell peppers, diced

½ cup zucchini, diced

1 Tbsp. garlic, minced

1 cup cooked garbanzo beans

½ tsp. ground cumin

½ tsp. curry powder

½ tsp. red pepper flakes

⅓ cup parsley, chopped

salt to taste

freshly ground pepper to taste

1. Place broth, 1 Tbsp. oil, and ¾ tsp. salt in large saucepan.

2. Cover and bring to boil.

3. Stir in couscous.

4. Cover and remove from heat. Allow to stand 5 minutes.

5. Uncover. Fluff couscous with fork. Set aside.

6. Meanwhile, place remaining oil in good-sized skillet over medium heat.

7. Add carrots, onions, peppers, zucchini, and garlic.

8. Sauté 5 minutes. Remove from heat.

9. Stir in beans, cumin, curry, and pepper flakes.

10. Season with salt and pepper.

11. Fold in couscous and parsley. Serve immediately.

Fresh Herb and Lemon Bulgur Pilaf

Janelle Glick

LANCASTER GENERAL WELLNESS PARTNERSHIP

Makes 6 servings
Prep. Time: 10–15 minutes ❧ *Cooking Time: 40 minutes*

2 Tbsp. extra-virgin olive oil

2 cups chopped onion

1 clove garlic, minced

1½ cups raw bulgur, preferably medium or coarse *

½ tsp. ground turmeric

½ tsp. ground cumin

2 cups vegetable broth, *or* reduced-sodium chicken broth

1½ cups chopped carrot

2 tsp. fresh ginger, grated *or* finely chopped

1 tsp. coarse salt

¼ cup lightly packed, finely chopped fresh dill

¼ cup lightly packed, finely chopped fresh mint

¼ cup lightly packed, finely chopped flat-leaf parsley

3 Tbsp. lemon juice, *or* more to taste

½ cup chopped walnuts, toasted **

1. In large high-sided skillet, or broad shallow saucepan, with tight-fitting lid, heat oil over medium heat until hot enough to sizzle a piece of onion.

2. Add onion. Reduce heat to medium-low, and cook, stirring often, until golden brown, about 12–18 minutes.

3. Stir in garlic and cook, stirring, for 1 minute.

4. Add bulgur, turmeric, and cumin. Cook, stirring, until bulgur is well coated with oil, about 1 minute.

5. Add broth, carrot, ginger, and salt. Bring to boil, stirring frequently.

recipe continues on the next page of text

**NOTE

To toast chopped walnuts, cook in a small dry skillet over medium-low heat, stirring constantly, until fragrant and lightly browned, 2–4 minutes.

* NOTE

Bulgur is made by parboiling, drying, and coarsely grinding or cracking wheat berries. Don't confuse bulgur with cracked wheat, which is simply that—cracked wheat. Since the parboiling step is skipped, cracked wheat must be cooked for up to an hour, whereas bulgur simply needs a quick soak in hot water for most uses. Look for it in the natural foods section of large supermarkets, near other grains.

6. Cover and cook over medium-low heat for about 15 minutes, or until broth is fully absorbed and there are "eyes" or indentations on the surface of the bulgur. *Do not stir the pilaf.*

7. Remove from heat and let stand, covered, 5 minutes.

8. Stir dill, mint, parsley, and lemon juice into pilaf.

9. Serve, topped with walnuts.

TIP

This pilaf may be covered and refrigerated for up to two days. Add more lemon juice and/or salt to taste before serving.

Rice Pilaf

Ruth Thomas
THOMAS PRODUCE

Makes 10-12 servings
Prep. Time: 15-20 minutes ❦ Cooking Time: 60-75 minutes

1 cup green onions, sliced
1 cup carrots, chopped
¾ stick (6 Tbsp.) butter
2½ cups raw long-grain rice
5 chicken bouillon cubes
1 small bay leaf
¼ tsp. salt
pinch of saffron, *optional*
4½ cups water
½ cup fresh parsley, chopped

1. In large saucepan, sauté onions and carrots in butter.

2. Add rice, bouillon cubes, bay leaf, salt, saffron if you wish, and water.

3. Stir all together.

4. Pour into greased 2½-3-quart baking dish.

5. Cover. Bake at 350° for 1 hour, or until rice is tender and water is absorbed.

6. Remove bay leaf before serving.

7. Stir in chopped parsley just before serving.

TIPS

1. *You can easily cut this recipe in half. Check after baking 45 minutes to see if rice is tender.*

2. *This is a dish that I often prepare for large family gatherings because it's so easy to fix and serve. It doesn't add to the last-minute pressure!*

Celery Stuffing

Trish Hillegas
SWEETHEARTS OF LANCASTER COUNTY

Makes 6 servings
Prep. Time: 20 minutes ❦ Cooking Time: 45 minutes

3–4 ribs celery
1 small onion
2 Tbsp. butter
1 quart dry bread crumbs
½ cup chicken broth
1½ tsp. parsley, fresh *or* dried
1½ tsp. dried oregano
1 tsp. salt
½ tsp. pepper
2 eggs, beaten

1. Chop celery and onion fine. Place in small bowl and set aside.

2. Melt butter and pour over bread crumbs in large mixing bowl.

3. Fold chicken broth into bread crumbs.

4. Fold in parsley, oregano, salt, and pepper.

5. Add eggs, celery and onion. Mix thoroughly.

6. Place in greased 2-quart baking dish. Bake, covered, at 350° for 30 minutes. Uncover and bake an additional 15 minutes to brown.

VARIATION

You can also use this as stuffing for chicken or turkey. Prepare according to instructions above through Step 5. Bake whatever doesn't fit in the bird in a greased baking dish, according to Step 6. You probably won't need to bake it quite as long as the recipe calls for. Check if it's heated through after baking 20 minutes. If so, remove cover and bake another 10 minutes to brown.

MAIN DISHES

Crispy Chicken

Bonnie Martin
SHENK'S POULTRY

Makes 8 servings
Prep. Time: 15–20 minutes ❧ Cooking Time: 30–70 minutes

1 cup grape-nuts cereal flakes
½ tsp. garlic salt
½ tsp. ground rosemary
⅛ tsp. pepper
2 Tbsp. vegetable oil
8 boneless, skinless chicken breast halves

1. Place cereal in blender. Cover and blend on low speed until cereal is finely crushed. Or pour it into a large zip-closure bag, close the bag, and crush the cereal with a rolling pin.

2. Mix cereal and seasonings in large bowl. Stir in oil until crumbs are evenly coated.

3. Dip each piece of chicken in water. Shake off excess water.

4. Dip each chicken piece in cereal mixture, turning to coat all sides evenly.

5. Place in foil-lined 10" × 15" baking pan.

6. Bake uncovered at 400° for 30–70 minutes, or until cooked through. (The wide range of baking times allows for pieces of different thicknesses and weight.)

Perfect Roast Chicken

Betsey Sterenfeld
CENTRAL MARKET CUSTOMER

Makes 4 servings ❦ *Prep. Time: 5 minutes*
Baking Time: 1–2 hours ❦ *Standing Time: 1 hour* ❦ *Resting Time: 10–15 minutes*

3–4-lb. whole fryer chicken
kosher salt
freshly ground black pepper
2 small lemons

TIPS

1. *Use a really fresh chicken.*

2. *The roasted chicken tastes great warm or cold.*

3. *Separate fat from pan juices. Then drizzle juices over chicken, bread, fingers, you name it!*
   In fact, my husband and I fight over the pan drippings when we're cleaning up.

1. Remove chicken from refrigerator 1 hour before cooking. Discard fat pads inside cavity.

2. Preheat oven to 400°.

3. Sprinkle generous amount of salt and black pepper on chicken, rubbing it with your fingers over entire body and into the cavity.

4. Using a fork, puncture each lemon in at least 20 places.

5. Place both lemons in bird's cavity.

6. Put chicken into lightly oiled roasting pan, uncovered, breast facing up. Place in upper third of preheated oven.

7. After 20 minutes, turn chicken over so that breast faces down. When turning it, try not to puncture the skin.

8. Roast for another 20 minutes. Turn chicken over with breast facing up and cook 20 more minutes.

9. Continue turning chicken over and roasting until meat is tender at joints and juices run clear.

10. Let chicken rest 10–15 minutes.

11. Remove lemons.

12. Carve chicken. Spoon juices over roasted pieces.

Buttermilk Roast Chicken

Donna Shenk
SHENK'S POULTRY

Makes 4 servings ❧ *Prep. Time: 15–20 minutes*
Marinating Time: 8 hours, or overnight ❧ *Cooking Time: about 65 minutes* ❧ *Resting Time: 10 minutes*

4-lb. chicken

2 cups buttermilk

6 Tbsp. vegetable oil, *divided*

2 cloves garlic, lightly crushed

1 Tbsp. crushed black peppercorns

1 Tbsp. sea salt

2 Tbsp. fresh rosemary leaves, roughly chopped

1 Tbsp. honey

1. Butterfly chicken by placing breast-side down. Using heavy-duty kitchen shears, cut along both sides of backbone. Or, ask your friendly butcher to do the job.

2. Discard backbone. Turn chicken over and open it like a book. Press gently to flatten.

3. Place chicken in large freezer bag. Add buttermilk, 4 Tbsp. oil, garlic, peppercorns, salt, rosemary, and honey.

4. Seal bag and refrigerate overnight.

5. When ready to roast chicken, heat oven to 400°.

6. Remove chicken from marinade and allow excess to drip off.

7. Line a roasting pan with foil. Place chicken in pan. Drizzle with remaining 2 Tbsp. oil.

8. Roast, uncovered, for 45 minutes.

9. Reduce heat to 325°. Continue roasting until meat is well browned and juices run clear when chicken is pierced where leg joins thigh, about another 20 minutes.

10. Allow to rest 10 minutes before cutting to serve.

Chicken Provencal With Pesto

Regine Ibold
THE SPICE STAND

Makes 6–8 servings ❦ *Prep. Time: 15 minutes* ❦ *Cooking Time: 1¾ hours*

Chicken Ingredients:

6 medium onions, coarsely chopped

½ cup olive oil

2 28-oz. cans plum tomatoes

1 Tbsp. fresh thyme *or* 1 tsp. dried thyme

1 Tbsp. fresh basil *or* 1 tsp. dried basil

1 Tbsp. fresh tarragon *or* 1 tsp. dried tarragon

1 Tbsp. fresh rosemary *or* 1 tsp. dried rosemary

4 cloves fresh garlic, minced

2–3-lb. chicken, cut up

2 cups chicken broth

4 cups dry white wine

1½–2 lbs. small new potatoes in skins

2 loaves French bread

Pesto Ingredients:

2 cups fresh basil *or* 2 Tbsp. dried basil

½ cup olive oil

2 Tbsp. pine nuts

2 cloves garlic, crushed

1 tsp. salt

½ cup Parmesan cheese, freshly grated

2 Tbsp. Romano cheese, grated

3 Tbsp. butter, softened

1. To prepare Pesto, blend all ingredients except cheeses and softened butter in a blender or food processor. Pour into a bowl and add cheeses and butter, mixing by hand.

2. In a Dutch oven sauté onions in olive oil until transparent. Add tomatoes with their juice. Add all herbs, garlic, chicken, broth, wine, and half of Pesto.

3. Cover and bake at 350° for 35 minutes. Add potatoes and bake 1 hour, or until potatoes are tender when pierced with a fork.

4. Serve in deep soup plates with plenty of hot French bread to mop up juices. Serve remaining Pesto at table.

 This is another peasant dish from Provence where cooking odors fill the house like perfume. Most of the dried herbs are available at my stand. Also available are the pine nuts for the all-time favorite Pesto which is great year-round on pasta or in soups.

— REGINE IBOLD, The Spice Stand

Cherry Chicken

Jim and Linda Kreider
COUNTRY MEADOWS

Makes 4–6 servings ❧ *Prep. Time: 30 minutes* ❧ *Baking Time: 1–1½ hours*

6–7-lb. chicken, cut-up

1 can dark Bing cherries in heavy syrup

1 tsp. dry mustard

2 Tbsp. cornstarch

½ cup brown sugar, packed

juice of 1 fresh lemon

orange juice added to lemon juice to make ½ cup juice

1. Preheat oven to 375°.

2. Arrange chicken pieces in greased 9"×13" baking dish.

3. Drain cherries. Reserve their liquid in saucepan.

4. Add dry mustard, cornstarch, brown sugar, and lemon and orange juices to cherry juice in saucepan.

5. Heat until thickened, stirring constantly.

6. Pour thickened liquid over chicken pieces.

7. Arrange cherries around chicken pieces.

8. Bake uncovered for 1–1½ hours, or until chicken is tender. Baste meat with juices every 20 minutes or so.

Japanese Marinade for Chicken Breasts

Bonnie Martin
SHENK'S POULTRY

Makes 4 servings ❧ *Prep. Time: 10 minutes* ❧ *Marinating Time: 3–6 hours*

½ cup canola oil

¼ cup rice wine vinegar

3 Tbsp. soy sauce

3 Tbsp. fresh ginger, chopped, *or* 1 tsp. ground ginger

2 Tbsp. sugar

4 chicken breast halves

1. Whisk all ingredients except chicken together in a mixing bowl.

2. Place chicken in shallow dish. Cover with marinade.

3. Cover dish and refrigerate for 3–6 hours.

4. Remove meat from marinade. Grill or broil chicken until no longer pink in center.

5. Discard leftover marinade.

Grilled Herbed Chicken

Gail Johnson
SLAYMAKER'S POULTRY

Makes 12-16 servings

Prep. Time: 15 minutes ❦ Cooking Time: 14-18 minutes ❦ Marinating Time: 2 hours, or overnight

½ cup olive oil

½ cup fresh lemon juice

1 tsp. Dijon mustard

4 cloves garlic, crushed

¼ cup fresh parsley, chopped

1 Tbsp. fresh rosemary, chopped

1 Tbsp. fresh tarragon, chopped

1 Tbsp. fresh sage, chopped

1 Tbsp. fresh oregano, chopped

1 Tbsp. fresh chives, chopped

½ tsp. salt

dash of fresh pepper

8 large, boneless, skinless chicken breasts, halved

1. Combine all ingredients except chicken in shallow dish. Add chicken breasts and marinate at least 2 hours, or overnight.

2. Grill or broil chicken for 7-9 minutes on each side, brushing with leftover marinade.

Honey Orange Teriyaki Chicken

Bonnie Martin
SHENK'S POULTRY

Makes 4-6 servings

Prep. Time: 10 minutes ❦ Marinating Time: 1-2 hours ❦ Cooking Time: 4-6 minutes

1 cup teriyaki sauce

1 cup orange juice

6 Tbsp. honey

1½ lbs. chicken breast, sliced, *or* chicken tenders

1 Tbsp. olive oil

1. Mix together teriyaki sauce, orange juice, and honey in a bowl.

2. Reserve 1 cup.

3. Place chicken in a single layer in a dish or baking pan. Pour sauce over top. Marinate chicken at least 1-2 hours.

4. Drain chicken and discard marinade.

5. Lightly brush grill pan with olive oil. Heat to medium.

6. Brush chicken with reserved marinade.

7. Cook 2–3 minutes.

8. Brush on additional marinade just before turning chicken over to cook other side. Cook an additional 2–3 minutes.

9. Use remaining reserved sauce at table as dipping sauce, or as salad dressing.

TIP

You can also make this recipe on a grill.

Greek Bandit-Style Chicken

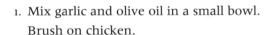

Sara Brandt
SIMPLY SWEET

Makes 4 servings
Prep. Time: 15 minutes ❧ *Cooking Time: 15 minutes*

1 Tbsp. minced garlic

3 Tbsp. olive oil

4 boneless, skinless chicken breast halves

salt and pepper to taste

1⅓ cups fully cooked red potatoes, diced

¼ cup crumbled feta cheese

1 lemon, thinly sliced

4 sprigs fresh oregano

VARIATION

Substitute dried oregano for the fresh sprigs and white potatoes for the red if you don't have the exact ingredients.

1. Mix garlic and olive oil in a small bowl. Brush on chicken.

2. Place each chicken breast in the middle of a square (big enough to completely wrap meat) of heavy-duty aluminum foil. Season with salt and pepper.

3. Top each breast with ⅓ cup diced potatoes, 1 Tbsp. crumbled feta, 2 slices of lemon and a sprig of oregano.

4. Wrap foil around each breast to create a pocket.

5. Put packets on the grill over medium heat.

6. Cover the grill and cook for 10–15 minutes, or until internal temperature of chicken is at least 165°.

Plantain and Chicken Curry

Betty Lichty
HORN OF PLENTY

Makes 4 servings
Prep. Time: 10 minutes ❧ Cooking Time: 30 minutes

4 chicken breasts

4 cups water

1 onion, sliced

1 medium apple, peeled and cut into cubes

4 Tbsp. butter

1 bay leaf

2 Tbsp. coconut flakes

3 tsp. curry powder

3 Tbsp. flour

salt and pepper to taste

½ pint heavy cream

1 ripe plantain (yellow skin with black spots), cubed

additional coconut flakes for garnish

1. Boil chicken breasts until tender in about 4 cups water. Remove chicken from broth; reserve 1½ cups broth. Cut chicken in bite-size cubes.

2. In a saucepan sauté onion and apple in butter. Add bay leaf, coconut flakes, and curry powder. Sprinkle with flour and sauté for 3 minutes. While stirring, add reserved broth.

3. When sauce is smooth, add salt and pepper to taste. Add cream, plantain, and chicken. Simmer for 10 minutes.

4. Serve over bed of rice and garnish with coconut flakes.

Green Curry Chicken

NARAI THAI CUISINE

Makes 3-4 servings
Prep. Time: 10 minutes Cooking Time: 20 minutes

1 lb. boneless, skinless chicken breast

2 Kaffir lime leaves

3 Tbsp. green curry paste

1 Tbsp. vegetable oil

1 can coconut milk

1 Tbsp. fish sauce

2 Tbsp. sugar

½ cup green beans, cut in half

½ cup red bell pepper, sliced into strips

½ cup bamboo strips

½ cup Thai basil

TIPS

1. *Add more green curry paste for a spicier flavor.*

2. *Instead of chicken, you can use tender beef, shrimp, or vegetables.*

1. Slice chicken into thin pieces. Set aside.

2. Chop lime leaves into small fine pieces. Set aside.

3. In small skillet, sauté green curry paste with vegetable oil over medium heat until smell of curry is evident.

4. Place coconut milk in good-sized saucepan and bring to a boil.

5. Stir sautéed curry paste into hot coconut milk.

6. Add fish sauce, sugar, and chopped kefir lime leaves.

7. Bring to boil. Stir in chicken.

8. Reduce heat. Add green beans, red peppers, and bamboo strips.

9. Turn off heat and sprinkle with basil.

10. Serve with cooked jasmine white rice.

Henner's Chicken Curry with Mushrooms and Spätzle

Henner and Heidi Steinle
THE GERMAN DELI

Makes 4-5 servings
Prep. Time: 25-30 minutes   *Cooking Time: 25-30 minutes*

half a stick (4 Tbsp.) butter, *or* margarine

4 boneless, skinless chicken breast halves, cut into bite-size pieces

1 tsp. salt

½ tsp. pepper

2 medium onions, finely sliced

½ lb. fresh mushrooms, sliced

4 Tbsp. flour

14½-oz. can chicken broth

2½ Tbsp. curry powder

½ cup white wine

2 cups sour cream

1 Tbsp. chopped parsley

8 oz. bag Spätzle

1. Melt butter or margarine in large skillet.

2. Add chicken, salt, and pepper.

3. Stir-fry just until chicken turns golden brown. Remove chicken from skillet. Set aside and keep warm.

4. Add onions and mushrooms to pan. Sauté 2 minutes.

5. Add chicken back into pan with onions. Dust mixture with flour.

6. Stir in chicken broth and curry. Bring to a boil.

7. Reduce heat to a simmer. Cook 10 minutes, stirring frequently.

8. Stir in wine and sour cream. Simmer 2-3 minutes.

9. Garnish with parsley.

10. Serve over Spätzle, prepared according to package directions.

TESTER TIP

This is also delicious served over cooked rice.

Chicken Stir-Fry

Ruth Harnish
SPRING GLEN

Makes 4 servings
Prep. Time: 20 minutes   Marinating Time: 30 minutes   Cooking Time: 15 minutes

1 lb. boneless, skinless chicken breasts

3 Tbsp. cornstarch

2 Tbsp. light soy sauce

½ tsp. ground ginger

¼ tsp. garlic powder

3 Tbsp. vegetable oil, *divided*

2 cups broccoli florets

1 cup celery, cut into ½"-thick slices

1 cup carrots, thinly sliced

1 small onion, cut into wedges

1 cup water

1 tsp. low sodium chicken bouillon granules

1. Cut chicken into ½"-wide strips. Place in zip-closure plastic bag.

2. Add cornstarch and toss to coat.

3. In a small bowl, combine soy sauce, ginger, and garlic powder. Add to bag and shake well.

4. Refrigerate for 30 minutes.

5. In a large skillet or wok, heat 2 Tbsp. oil.

6. Stir-fry chicken until no longer pink, about 3–5 minutes. Remove and keep warm.

7. Add remaining oil to skillet. Stir-fry broccoli, celery, carrots, and onions 4–5 minutes, or until crisp-tender.

8. Add water and bouillon.

9. Return chicken to skillet.

10. Cook and stir until thickened and bubbly.

11. Serve over rice.

Bruschetta Chicken Bake

Joyce Denlinger
S. CLYDE WEAVER, INC.

Makes 6 servings
Prep. Time: 10 minutes 🌿 Cooking Time: 30–40 minutes

14½-oz. can seasoned diced tomatoes, undrained

6-oz. pkg. stuffing mix for chicken

½ cup water

1½ lbs. boneless, skinless chicken breasts, cut into bite-size pieces

1 tsp. dried basil

1 cup mozzarella cheese, shredded

1. Preheat oven to 400°.

2. Place tomatoes in good-sized mixing bowl.

3. Add stuffing mix and water. Stir just until stuffing mix is moistened. Set aside.

4. Place chicken in 9" × 9" or 3-quart baking dish.

5. Sprinkle with basil and cheese.

6. Top with stuffing mixture.

7. Bake, uncovered, 30–40 minutes, or until chicken is cooked thoroughly.

TESTER TIP

For added flavor, stir ½ cup chopped celery and 1 tsp. soy sauce into Step 3.

I have always loved going to market. My dad would call us as he left the house to load the market truck. We had an understanding with him that if the kitchen light was on when he drove back past the house, he would wait for us to come out and go with him. My mother says we were grouchy all day if we didn't make it out of bed in time to turn on that light.

— SAM NEFF, S. Clyde Weaver, Inc.

Sour Cream Chicken

Darla Lamoureux
WILLOW VALLEY BAKERY

Makes 8 servings

Prep: Time: 10 minutes ❧ Standing Time: overnight ❧ Baking Time: 55 minutes

1 cup sour cream

2 Tbsp. lemon juice

2 tsp. Worcestershire sauce

1 tsp. paprika

1½ tsp. salt

¼ tsp. pepper

4 chicken breasts, split, boned and skinned

1 cup fine bread crumbs

½ cup margarine, melted

1. Combine all ingredients except chicken breasts, bread crumbs, and margarine. Mix well.

2. Coat chicken breasts with this mixture and let stand overnight, covered.

3. Roll chicken in bread crumbs. Place chicken pieces in a baking dish. Spoon ¼ cup melted margarine over chicken. Bake uncovered at 325° for 40 minutes.

4. Spoon remaining margarine over chicken and bake 15 minutes longer.

5. Serve over rice or noodles.

NOTE

This recipe is easy to prepare the day before an elegant dinner party!

Amish Roast

Edith Groff
GROFF'S HOMEGROWN VEGETABLES

Makes 12–15 servings ❧ *Prep. Time: 20 minutes*
Cooking Time: 1–1½ hours ❧ *Baking Time: 1–1½ hours* ❧ *Cooling Time: 30 minutes*

3–4 lbs. chicken pieces
(enough to yield 4 cups diced,
cooked chicken)

2 sticks (12–16 Tbsp.) butter

1 medium onion, chopped

1 cup diced celery

1 tsp. salt

1 tsp. dried basil

4 eggs, beaten

3 cups milk

1 cup chicken broth

18–20 slices bread, cubed
(about 12 cups)

NOTE

To prepare gravy, pour 1 cup cold water into jar with tight-fitting lid. Add ½ cup plus 2 Tbsp. flour to water. Shake vigorously until well blended.

In a medium-sized saucepan bring 4 cups chicken broth to a boil. Slowly stir in flour water while broth simmers gently. Stir constantly until gravy thickens and becomes smooth.

1. Place chicken in stockpot. Add water so that chicken pieces are just covered.

2. Cover pot and simmer until chicken is tender, about 1–1½ hours.

3. Remove chicken from pot. Reserve broth.

4. When chicken has cooled enough to handle, debone and cut up into bite-sized chunks.

5. Measure out 1 cup broth. Make gravy with the remaining broth (see Note below), or freeze it for a future use.

6. Melt butter in saucepan. Sauté onion and celery.

7. Stir in salt and basil. Set sautéed and seasoned vegetables aside.

8. In a large bowl, combine eggs, milk, and 1 cup broth. Gently stir in bread cubes until they're evenly moistened.

9. Stir in sautéed vegetables and chicken.

10. Spread into a greased 9" × 13" baking pan. Bake uncovered at 350° for 1–1½ hours. If Roast begins to darken toward end of baking time, cover with foil.

Happy Hen Stew

ORGANIC ACRES

Makes 6 servings
Prep. Time: 20 minutes ❧ Cooking Time: 1¾ hours

1 large pastured chicken
2 cups water
1 cup tomato juice
1 large onion, quartered
3 celery tops
3 celery ribs, cut into 1" pieces
1 bay leaf
5 carrots, sliced into coins, *divided*
1 large tomato, diced
1 large green bell pepper, diced
1½ cups uncooked brown rice
1 cup small mushrooms
1 tsp. curry powder
pinch of dried tarragon
tomato juice

1. Cut chicken into serving pieces.

2. In large kettle or Dutch oven, simmer chicken with 2 cups water, 1 cup tomato juice, onion, celery tops and pieces, bay leaf, and 1 sliced carrot for 45 minutes.

3. Remove chicken pieces to a warm platter. Strain broth and skim off fat.

4. Return chicken pieces and broth to kettle.

5. Add remaining carrots, along with tomato, green pepper, brown rice, mushrooms, curry powder, and tarragon.

6. Add additional water and tomato juice to cover.

7. Cook an additional hour, or until rice is soft and chicken is tender.

Healthy Cordon Bleu Bake

Thelma Thomas
SPRING GLEN

Makes 6 servings
Prep. Time: 30 minutes ❦ Cooking Time: 50 minutes

¾ cup bread crumbs

½ tsp. onion powder

½ tsp. garlic powder

½ tsp. black pepper

2 lbs. boneless, skinless, chicken breasts, cut in ½" pieces

3 Tbsp. butter

3 Tbsp. flour

1 tsp. salt

dash of pepper

2½ cups fat-free milk

1½ cups lean ham, diced

1 cup Swiss cheese, grated

4–6 cups fresh, *or* frozen, thawed, broccoli, cut into bite-size pieces

1. Preheat oven to 375°.

2. Spray a baking sheet and a 2-quart baking dish with non-stick cooking spray. Set both aside.

3. Place bread crumbs in a shallow bowl.

4. Stir in onion, garlic powder, and pepper.

5. Drop the chicken pieces in batches into bread crumbs to coat.

6. Place on baking sheet. Spray with cooking oil. Bake 10 minutes.

7. Turn chicken over and spray other side. Bake another 10 minutes.

8. While chicken is baking, melt butter in medium-sized saucepan. Stir in flour, salt, and dash of pepper. Cook over low heat, stirring constantly, for 1 minute.

9. Gradually stir in milk. Stir until sauce begins to simmer. Continue stirring until sauce thickens and is smooth.

10. Remove chicken to baking dish.

11. Layer ham, cheese, and broccoli into baking dish on top of chicken.

12. Pour sauce over baking dish ingredients.

13. Reduce oven to 350°. Bake uncovered for 30 minutes.

Hungarian Chicken Livers

Cindy Cover
MARION CHEESE

Makes 4-6 servings
Prep. Time: 10 minutes   Cooking Time: 20-25 minutes

5 slices bacon

1 large green pepper, chopped

1 large onion, chopped

¾ lb. fresh mushrooms, cleaned and sliced

2 Tbsp. hot Hungarian paprika

1½ lbs. chicken livers

1 cup sour cream

cooked rice or noodles

NOTE

I love chicken livers and enjoy finding ways to dress them up.

1. Fry bacon in large skillet. Remove, crumble, and reserve.

2. Pour all except ¼ cup bacon drippings from pan. Add chopped peppers and onions and sauté until golden. Add mushrooms and paprika and sauté a few minutes longer.

3. Rinse chicken livers. Pat dry. Add chicken livers to skillet and sauté over high heat until cooked through.

4. Remove from heat. Add bacon and sour cream. Return to burner and heat gently. Do not boil.

5. Serve over rice or noodles.

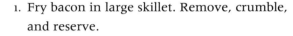 *The best thing about working with my father, Chester Thomas, was the way he gave us responsibilities. He did not order us around. Rather he made us responsible for certain jobs even when we were young boys.*

— ERNIE THOMAS, C. H. Thomas and Sons

Easy Chicken Enchiladas

Bonnie Martin
SHENK'S POULTRY

Makes 5 servings
Prep. Time: 15–20 minutes ❦ *Baking Time: 20–30 minutes*

8-oz. can enchilada sauce, *divided*

half an 8-oz. block of cream cheese, cubed

1½ cups salsa

2 cups cooked chicken, cubed

15½-oz. can pinto beans, rinsed and drained

4-oz. can green chilies, chopped

10 6" flour tortillas

1 cup shredded Mexican blend cheese

shredded lettuce, chopped

1 large tomato, chopped

sour cream

1. Spoon ½ cup enchilada sauce into a greased 9"×13" baking pan.

2. In large saucepan, cook and stir cream cheese and salsa together over medium heat for 2–3 minutes.

3. Stir in chicken, beans, and chilies.

4. Place about 6 Tbsp. chicken mixture down center of each tortilla.

5. Roll up and place seam-side down over sauce in baking pan.

6. Spoon remaining enchilada sauce over filled enchiladas.

7. Sprinkle evenly with cheese.

8. Cover and bake at 350° for 20–30 minutes, or until heated through.

9. Serve topped with lettuce, tomato, and sour cream.

Caesar Chicken Wraps

Dawn Meck
MECK'S PRODUCE

Makes 5 servings
Prep. Time: 25 minutes ❦ *Cooking Time: 15 minutes*

½ cup Caesar salad dressing

½ cup shredded Parmesan cheese, *divided*

1 tsp. lemon juice

1 minced garlic clove

¼ tsp. pepper

8-oz. pkg. cream cheese, softened

3 cups romaine lettuce, torn

½ cup diced sweet red bell peppers

2¼-oz. can sliced black olives, drained

5 flour tortillas

2 cups cooked chicken, shredded

1. In a small bowl, combine Caesar dressing, ¼ cup Parmesan cheese, lemon juice, garlic, and pepper.

2. Set aside.

3. In a mixing bowl, beat cream cheese until smooth.

4. Mix ½ cup salad dressing mixture into cream cheese. Save for wrap assembly.

5. In a separate mixing bowl, combine lettuce, peppers, and olives.

6. Toss with remaining salad dressing mix.

7. Warm tortillas.

8. Spread each tortilla with approximately ¼ cup cream cheese mixture.

9. Top each with about ½ cup veggie mix and about ⅓ cup cooked, shredded chicken.

10. Sprinkle each with about 2 tsp. Parmesan cheese. Wrap securely.

11. Repeat for each tortilla.

Super Stuffed Tortillas

Janelle and Kendal Yoder

LETTUCE TOSS SALAD

Makes 6-8 servings

Prep. Time: 30 minutes ❧ Cooking Time: about 5 minutes per tortilla

1-2 garlic cloves, minced

4 tsp. oil, *divided*

1 large onion, chopped

1 green bell pepper, chopped

2 cups corn

1 small-medium zucchini, sliced

12½-oz. can cooked chicken, *or turkey, optional*

1½ tsp. ground cumin

2 cups black beans, cooked

1 cup chicken, *or* vegetable, broth

6 tsp. salsa

½–¾ tsp. salt, according to your taste preference

¼–½ tsp. freshly ground black pepper, according to your taste preference

½ cup sliced green onions

flour, *or* corn, tortillas

1½ cups cheddar, *or* mozzarella, cheese, shredded

freshly ground pepper

1. In a large skillet, sauté garlic in 2 tsp. oil for 1 minute.

2. Add onion and green pepper.

3. Sauté until crisp-tender.

4. Add corn, zucchini, chicken or turkey if you wish, and cumin.

5. Continue to sauté until all vegetables are tender but not browned.

6. Add beans, broth, and salsa.

7. Cook, stirring frequently, until there is no excess moisture.

8. Remove from heat. Add salt, pepper, and sliced green onions.

9. Set vegetable mixture aside.

10. Preheat skillet with remaining 2 tsp. oil.

11. Place one tortilla in skillet.

12. Add about ¼ cup shredded cheese in center of tortilla.

13. Add ¼–½ cup vegetables to tortilla. Season with pepper.

14. When tortilla is crispy, after about 5 minutes, remove and fold in half. Keep warm while preparing rest of tortillas.

Turkey Herb Steak Marinade

Roger Shenk
SHENK'S POULTRY

Makes about 1¼ cups ❧ *Prep. Time: 5–10 minutes*
Marinading Time: 30 minutes–12 hours ❧ *Grilling/Broiling Time: 16–20 minutes*

½ cup dry red wine

¼ cup olive oil

2 tsp. Worcestershire sauce

2 tsp. dried Italian seasoning, *or*
1 tsp. dried basil and 1 tsp. dried
oregano

1½ tsp. garlic powder

1 tsp. seasoning salt

1 tsp. coarse black pepper

1½ lbs. turkey London broil *or*
turkey cutlet

1. Combine all ingredients except turkey in a sturdy, self-closing plastic bag. Mix well.

2. Add turkey to marinade in bag. Gently squish the marinade around the turkey so it's fully surrounded by the liquid.

3. Place filled plastic bag in a low dish with sides (in case the bag leaks). Refrigerate for at least 30 minutes, or up to 12 hours. Turn meat occasionally.

4. Lightly grease grill rack. Preheat grill to medium heat. Or, turn on broiler.

5. Grill or broil 8–10 minutes per side, or until meat is no longer pink in center. (Cut a slash into the thickest part of the meat to check.) Grilling time will vary depending on thickness of steak and temperature of grill or broiler.

6. When meat is finished, slice thin at a 45° angle and serve. Discard marinade.

Sausage and Three-Cheese Macaroni and Cheese

Linda Rittenhouse
TURKEY LADY

Makes 10–12 servings
Prep. Time: 25 minutes ❧ Cooking Time: 20 minutes

1-lb. box short pasta (elbow, cavatappi, *or* pipette)

2 Tbsp. extra-virgin olive oil

¾ lb. bulk sweet Italian turkey sausage

1 small yellow onion, chopped

4 large cloves garlic, chopped

salt and pepper to taste

3 Tbsp. flour

1 cup chicken stock

3 cups milk, *or* half-and-half

pinch of nutmeg (a few passes on the grater)

1½ cups Asiago cheese, grated

2 cups provolone cheese, grated

2 cups stuffing bread cubes

half a stick (4 Tbsp.) butter, melted

½ cup Parmigiano, *or* Reggiano cheese, grated

½ cup flat-leaf parsley leaves, chopped

1. Cook pasta al dente according to package directions.

2. Drain and reserve.

3. While preparing pasta, heat olive oil in very large skillet over medium-high heat.

4. Add sausage, breaking it up into small pieces with back of a wooden spoon as it cooks.

5. When brown, remove sausage from skillet. Drain off all but 3 Tbsp. drippings.

6. Return skillet to heat and add onions and garlic. Season with salt and pepper.

7. Cook, stirring frequently, until onions start to soften.

8. Sprinkle onions with flour and continue to cook another minute.

9. Whisk in chicken stock and milk. Bring to a simmer, stirring frequently, and season with nutmeg.

10. Continue stirring until mixture thickens.

11. Gradually stir in Asiago and provolone cheeses. Continue stirring until melted.

12. Add drained pasta and cooked sausage to cheese sauce, stirring to combine.

13. Transfer to large, greased baking dish.

14. Preheat broiler on high.

15. In a bowl, combine bread crumbs, melted butter, Parmigiano, and chopped parsley.

16. Toss to combine, and then sprinkle over baking dish contents.

17. Place baking dish under broiler. Broil until bread topping browns. Watch carefully so it doesn't burn!

Easy Turkey Parmigiana

Joyce G. Slaymaker
SLAYMAKER'S POULTRY

Makes 4 servings
Prep. Time: 5 minutes ❧ Cooking Time: 5-10 minutes ❧ Baking Time: 40 minutes

4 turkey breast fillets
1 egg, slightly beaten
½ cup bread crumbs
2 Tbsp. oil
¼ cup onion, minced
1 cup tomato sauce *or* spaghetti sauce
4 oz. mozzarella cheese, sliced *or* shredded
grated Parmesan cheese, *optional*

1. Dip turkey fillets into egg, and then into bread crumbs.

2. Brown slowly in oil.

3. Arrange fillets in a baking dish. Sprinkle onion on top and add tomato sauce.

4. Bake uncovered at 350° for 30 minutes.

5. Top with cheese and bake 10 minutes longer.

Best Barbecue Sauce

Joanne Warfel
S. CLYDE WEAVER, INC.

Makes about 1¼ cups
Prep Time: 5–10 minutes   Cooking Time: 10–15 minutes

Sauce:
1 cup ketchup
½ cup brown sugar, packed
⅓ cup sugar
¼ cup honey
¼ cup molasses
2 tsp. prepared regular mustard
1½ tsp. Worcestershire sauce
¼ tsp. liquid smoke
¼ tsp. salt
⅛ tsp. pepper

1. Combine sauce ingredients in small saucepan.

2. Bring to a boil, stirring occasionally. Remove from heat.

3. Serve with burgers instead of plain ketchup.

VARIATION

If you wish, use ¼ cup Best Barbecue Sauce as an ingredient in Favorite Turkey Burgers (page 87), instead of ¼ cup Dijon mustard – or use the Sauce to replace an equivalent amount of tomato juice or milk in any other burger recipe.

Turkey Sausage Cabbage Dinner

Faye Hess
WILLOW VALLEY BAKERY

Makes 4-6 servings
Prep. Time: 30 minutes   Cooking Time: 8-9 hours

1 medium head cabbage
6–8 medium potatoes
2 lbs. turkey sausage
½ tsp. salt
¼ tsp. pepper
1 quart water

1. Cut cabbage into wedges.

2. Place in slow cooker.

3. Wash and quarter potatoes, but do not peel.

4. Mix into cabbage in slow cooker.

5. Cut sausage into bite-sized pieces. Add to slow cooker with salt and pepper.

6. Add water and mix well together.

7. Cook on High for 2 hours.

8. Turn slow cooker to Low. Cook 6–7 more hours, or until vegetables are tender.

Favorite Turkey Burgers

Susan Glouner
TURKEY LADY

Makes 4-6 servings
Prep. Time: 10 minutes ❧ Cooking Time: 22-24 minutes

1½ lbs. ground turkey

½ cup finely-grated Gruyere cheese

4 thinly sliced scallions

¼ cup dried bread crumbs

¼ cup Dijon mustard

1 minced clove garlic

¾ tsp. salt

¼–½ tsp. pepper

VARIATION

If you wish, replace ¼ cup Dijon mustard with ¼ cup Best Barbecue Sauce (page 86) in the Turkey Burgers.

1. Heat grill to high.

2. Gently combine all ingredients in a medium-sized bowl.

3. Form mixture into 1"-thick patties.

4. Lightly oil grill.

5. Place patties on hottest part of grill.

6. Sear until brown, 1–2 minutes per side.

7. Move patties to cooler part of grill.

8. Continue grilling until cooked through, 5 to 10 minutes per side.

9. Serve with your favorite condiments and sandwich rolls.

Applesauce Meat Loaf

Eugene A. Martin
S. CLYDE WEAVER, INC.

Makes 3-4 servings   ❧   *Prep. Time: 15 minutes*   ❧   *Cooking Time: 45 minutes–1 hour*

1 lb. ground beef
1 egg, beaten
2 Tbsp. chopped onion
1 tsp. salt
½ cup bread, *or* cracker, crumbs
½ cup applesauce
2 Tbsp. ketchup

1. Combine beef, egg, onion, salt, crumbs, and applesauce.

2. Mix well. Shape into loaf and place in loaf-shaped baking pan.

3. Spread ketchup on top of loaf.

4. Bake at 350° for 1 hour.

Little Cheddar Meat Loaves

Ruth Harnish
SPRING GLEN

Makes 8 servings   ❧   *Prep. Time: 15 minutes*   ❧   *Cooking Time: 45 minutes*

1 egg
¾ cup milk
1 cup (4 ozs.) cheddar cheese, shredded
½ cup dry quick-cooking oats
½ cup chopped onions
1 tsp. salt
1 lb. lean ground beef
⅔ cup ketchup
½ cup packed brown sugar
1½ tsp. prepared mustard

1. In a good-sized mixing bowl beat egg and milk together.

2. Stir in cheese, oats, onions, and salt.

3. Add beef and mix well.

4. Shape into eight loaves.

5. Place in a greased 9"×13" baking dish.

6. In a small bowl, combine ketchup, brown sugar, and mustard.

7. Spoon over loaves.

8. Bake uncovered at 350° for 45 minutes.

Swedish Meatballs (Köttbullar)

Henner and Heide Steinle
THE GERMAN DELI

Makes 4 servings
Prep. Time: 30 minutes ❦ Cooking Time: 20 minutes

1 lb. ground beef

¼ tsp. salt

⅛ tsp. pepper

2 tsp. vegetable oil

½ lb. fresh white mushrooms

1 envelope Köttbullar mix, *or* dry onion soup mix

¾ cup water

¼ cup heavy cream

TIP

These are great served over buttered noodles or mashed potatoes.

1. In a mixing bowl combine beef, salt, and pepper.

2. Shape into 1" balls.

3. Place in a large skillet with vegetable oil.

4. Brown, stirring occasionally until browned all over, about 6 minutes.

5. Add mushrooms. Cook for an additional 1-3 minutes, stirring continually until mushrooms begin to soften.

6. Move meatballs to side of skillet.

7. Combine soup mix, water, and cream in bowl. Stir into skillet.

8. Continue stirring until mixture boils.

9. Reduce heat and simmer 5 more minutes.

Spaghetti Sauce with Curry

Arlene Leaman
S. CLYDE WEAVER, INC.

Makes 15-20 servings ❧ *Prep. Time: 20 minutes* ❧ *Cooking Time: 2½-3 hours*

1 large onion, chopped

equal amount of celery (as onion), chopped

half a stick (4 Tbsp.) butter

1 tsp. pepper

1 tsp. nutmeg

3 tsp. curry powder

1½ tsp. dried oregano

3 tsp. salt

3 tsp. brown sugar

1 cup milk

3 lbs. hamburger

2½ qts., *or* 3 1-lb.10-oz. jars, spaghetti sauce; homemade, *or* your favorite store-bought variety

6-oz. can tomato paste

1. In a large stockpot, sauté onion and celery in butter.

2. Stir in pepper, nutmeg, curry powder, oregano, salt, brown sugar, milk, and hamburger. Stir frequently, breaking up hamburger with a wooden spoon.

3. When well mixed, cover and simmer together for 2½-3 hours.

4. One half hour before serving, stir in spaghetti sauce and tomato paste.

5. Let simmer uncovered until ready to serve.

6. Serve over spaghetti.

Barbecued London Broil

Mike Bell
M.E. BELL, INC.

Makes 4 servings

Prep. Time: 5 minutes ❧ *Marinating Time: 4 hours, or overnight* ❧ *Cooking Time: 13-17 minutes*

¾ cup Italian-style salad dressing

1 tsp. Worcestershire sauce

1 tsp. dry mustard

¼ tsp. thyme

1 medium onion, sliced

1. Combine all ingredients except steak.

2. Place steak in a shallow dish and pour marinade over top. Cover and refrigerate at least 4 hours, or overnight.

2 Tbsp. butter, melted

1½ lbs. flank steak, scored,
or top round, scored

3. Remove steak from marinade. Grill over hot coals for 5 minutes on each side. Occasionally brush marinade over top. Steak may also be broiled in oven, 3–4" from heat for 5–7 minutes on each side.

4. Onions from marinade may be sautéed in skillet over hot coals or on top of stove for about 3 minutes.

5. To serve, slice steak in thin, diagonal slices across the grain. Sprinkle onions on top.

Stuffed Acorn Squash

Ethel Stoner
STONER'S VEGETABLES

Makes 4 servings
Prep. Time: 10 minutes ❧ *Cooking Time: 50 minutes*

2 acorn squash, halved
and seeded

1 lb. ground beef, *or*
ground turkey

½ cup apple, chopped

1 tsp. curry powder

½ lb. cheese, cubed

2 Tbsp. marmalade, *or*
apricot preserves

½–¾ tsp. salt, according
to your taste preference

1 cup apples, sliced thin

1 Tbsp. butter

¼ tsp. cinnamon

¼ tsp. nutmeg

1. Place squash in lightly greased baking dish, cut-side down. Bake at 400° for 35–40 minutes, or until tender.

2. Meanwhile, brown beef in skillet. Drain off drippings.

3. Stir chopped apples and curry powder into beef. Cook until tender.

4. Add cheese, preserves, and salt, stirring occasionally until cheese is melted.

5. In a separate skillet, sauté apple slices in butter until just-tender. Season lightly with cinnamon and nutmeg.

6. Remove squash from oven. Place on serving plates. Fill cavities with meat mixture. Top with sautéed apples.

Steak Marinade

Margie Shaffer
S. CLYDE WEAVER, INC.

Makes 1¼ cups

Prep. Time: 5 minutes ❧ *Marinating Time: 4–8 hours, or overnight*

¼ cup packed brown sugar

2 Tbsp. olive oil

¾ cup soy sauce

¼ cup white vinegar

3 Tbsp. Worcestershire sauce

1 tsp. ground ginger

1. Combine all ingredients in bowl.

2. Place in large zip-closure bag with steaks of your choice.

3. Cover and marinate a minimum of 4 hours in refrigerator.

4. Grill steaks until done to your liking, basting with marinade while grilling.

5. Discard leftover marinade.

Company Beef

Cynthia Strube
MARION CHEESE

Makes 4 servings

Prep. Time: 10 minutes ❧ *Cooking Time: 10 minutes* ❧ *Baking Time: 2½ hours*

2 thick slices slab bacon

1½-lb. chuck roast

salt and pepper to taste

1 cup flour

2 large cloves garlic

1 cup dry red wine

1 cup beef broth *or* beef bouillon

1 large onion

1. Cut bacon into pieces and cook in small roaster or Dutch oven.

2. Cut chuck roast into bite-size pieces. Salt and pepper and dredge in flour. Remove bacon pieces from roaster. Add beef to bacon drippings and brown. Add garlic. Add wine and broth, stirring to loosen any bits from bottom of roaster.

recipe continues on the next page of text

2 large tomatoes
1 lb. miniature new potatoes
1 tsp. nutmeg
1½ tsp. thyme
1 Tbsp. parsley

3. Chop onion and tomatoes. Add all remaining ingredients to roaster. Return bacon pieces to roaster and stir mixture thoroughly.

4. Cover and bake at 325° for 2½ hours. After 1½ hours, taste. Adjust salt and pepper to taste.

NOTE

Served with crusty bread and green salad, this hearty, flavorful stew is great for cold winter evenings or tailgate parties.

Pastured Meat Barbecue Sauce

ORGANIC ACRES

Makes 2 cups
Prep. Time: 10 minutes ❦ Cooking Time: 25 minutes

¼ cup apple cider vinegar
½ cup water
2 Tbsp. sugar
1 Tbsp. prepared mustard
½ tsp. freshly ground black pepper
¼ tsp. cayenne pepper
1 tsp. salt, preferably sea salt
1 Tbsp. lemon juice
1 medium onion, sliced
¼ cup butter, *or* olive oil
½ cup ketchup
2 Tbsp. Worcestershire sauce
1½ tsp. liquid smoke

1. Mix vinegar, water, sugar, mustard, peppers, salt, lemon juice, onion, and butter together in a saucepan.

2. Simmer uncovered for 20 minutes.

3. Add ketchup, Worcestershire sauce, and liquid smoke.

4. Bring to boil.

5. Serve as a topping for hamburgers or grilled chicken, or mix into pulled pork or beef.

Cottage Ham and String Beans

Regine Ibold
THE SPICE STAND

Makes 6-8 servings

Prep. Time: 10 minutes ❧ Soaking Time: 1 hour ❧ Cooking Time: 65 minutes

1½ lbs. yellow string beans

1½ lbs. green string beans (or use all green beans)

1 red onion, chopped

1 carrot, chopped

3 cloves garlic, peeled but left whole

¼ cup olive oil

2–3-lb. boneless pork shoulder butt

2 lbs. fresh plum tomatoes, *or* 2 lbs. canned tomatoes, drained

2 Tbsp. fresh basil leaves, *or* 2 tsp. dried basil leaves

salt and pepper to taste

1. Snap ends of beans and soak in cold water for 1 hour.

2. In Dutch oven sauté onion, carrot and garlic in olive oil until soft.

3. Add string beans and nestle meat in middle.

4. Top with plum tomatoes and basil leaves. Add salt and pepper to taste. Do not add water (beans shed their own liquid).

5. Cook covered 1 hour, or until ham is cooked through.

Apricot Ham Glaze With Mustard Sauce

Sam and Nancy Neff
S. CLYDE WEAVER, INC.

Makes 12-16 servings

Prep. Time: 15 minutes ❧ Baking Time: 3 hours

Ham Ingredients:

8–10-lb. ham

cloves

½ cup apricot jam

2 Tbsp. cider vinegar

2 Tbsp. spicy mustard

1. Score ham. Dot with cloves.

2. Mix jam, vinegar, and mustard together.

3. With the fattier side up, spread ½ of jam mixture over top of ham. Bake at 325° for 1½ hours.

Mustard Sauce Ingredients:
6–8 Tbsp. maple syrup
½ cup spicy mustard

VARIATION

Use peach jam instead of apricot jam.

4. Reglaze and bake an additional hour.

5. Reglaze and bake an additional ½ hour.

6. To prepare mustard sauce, mix maple syrup with ½ cup mustard. Serve with baked ham.

Asparagus and Ham Pie

Sue Eshleman

Makes 6-8 servings
Prep. Time: 10 minutes ❧ *Cooking Time: 30 minutes* ❧ *Broiling Time: 5 minutes*

1½ lbs. fresh asparagus, cut into 1" lengths
2 Tbsp. butter
¼ cup flour
¼ tsp. salt
dash of pepper
2 cups milk, *or* half-and-half
2 Tbsp. mayonnaise
2 Tbsp. lemon juice
½ lb. cooked ham, cut in cubes
9" baked pie shell
¼ cup Parmesan cheese

TIP

You can also serve the asparagus and ham in white sauce over toast cubes or toasted English muffins.

1. Steam or cook asparagus just until done. Drain.

2. Prepare white sauce by melting butter in saucepan. Stir in flour, salt, and pepper. Cook for a minute or two.

3. Gradually stir in milk or half-and-half. Continue stirring over low heat as mixture begins to simmer.

4. When sauce has thickened, add mayonnaise and lemon juice to white sauce. Stir until well combined.

5. Add ham cubes and asparagus.

6. Pour into baked pie shell.

7. Sprinkle with Parmesan cheese.

8. Broil just until cheese starts to brown. Watch carefully to prevent burning.

Henner's Pork Schnitzel with Potato Dumplings and Red Cabbage

Henner and Heidi Steinle
THE GERMAN DELI

Makes 4 servings
Prep. Time: 25-30 minutes ❧ Cooking Time: 25-30 minutes

4 boneless loin of pork cutlets, ½"-thick

½ cup flour

¾ tsp. salt

¼ tsp. pepper

2 eggs

1 Tbsp. water

1 cup plain bread crumbs, or more as needed

½ cup vegetable oil

1 jar prepared red cabbage, undrained

2 pkgs. potato dumplings

1 package Jägersauce

1 stick (8 Tbsp.) butter

⅓ cup bread crumbs

slices of lemon

1. Pound cutlets between sheets of plastic to ¼" thickness.

2. Mix flour with salt and pepper in a shallow bowl.

3. Place eggs in another shallow bowl. Beat, and then stir in water.

4. Place 1 cup bread crumbs in a third shallow bowl.

5. Dip cutlets to coat both sides evenly, first in seasoned flour, then in egg mixture, and finally in bread crumbs.

6. Press crumb coating firmly into cutlets.

7. Meanwhile, heat oil in large skillet over medium heat.

8. Add cutlets, 1 or 2 at a time to hot skillet. Do not crowd the pan or the cutlets will steam rather than brown.

9. Cook cutlets 2-3 minutes per side until browned. When finished, remove to a large platter and keep warm. Repeat browning process until all cutlets are finished.

10. Meanwhile, heat red cabbage in small saucepan.

11. Prepare potato dumplings as directed.

12. Prepare Jägersauce according to package directions.

13. Melt butter in saucepan. Stir in ⅓ cup bread crumbs. Sauté until crumbs brown.

14. Surround cutlets on platter with heated cabbage and prepared dumplings.

15. Sprinkle browned bread crumbs over dumplings.

16. Garnish platter with lemon slices.

17. Pass prepared Jägersauce around the table for drizzling over cutlets.

Henner's Sauerkraut with Kasseler (Smoked Pork Chops)

Heidi and Henner Steinle
THE GERMAN DELI

Makes 4 servings
Prep. Time: 10 minutes ❧ Cooking Time: 60–70 minutes

1 Tbsp. bacon fat

medium-sized apple, peeled, cored, and sliced thin

medium-sized onion, peeled and sliced thin

15½-oz. can sauerkraut, undrained

10–12 juniper berries

1 tsp. caraway seed

1 cup water

4 Kasseler ribs (smoked pork chops) about ¾" thick

6 Tbsp. white wine

1. In a large saucepan place bacon fat, apple, and onion slices. Heat over medium heat until translucent, stirring frequently.

2. Add sauerkraut, juniper berries, caraway seeds, and 1 cup water.

3. Cover and simmer 30 minutes, or until sauerkraut is softened to your liking.

4. Add Kasseler (chops) on top of sauerkraut.

5. Cover and simmer until heated through, 20–30 more minutes.

6. Add wine at end of cooking time.

Sausage and Pepper Penne

Margie Shaffer
S. CLYDE WEAVER, INC.

Makes 8–10 servings
Prep. Time: 20 minutes ❧ Cooking Time: 30 minutes

2 lbs. fresh sausage, cut into 2" pieces

2 Tbsp. olive oil

1 yellow, *or* red, bell pepper, cut in strips

1 onion, cut in wedges

1-lb. box penne pasta

1 bunch broccoli, cut up

1 tomato, cut into chunks

2 Tbsp. balsamic vinegar

¼ tsp. red pepper flakes

½ cup grated Parmesan cheese

1. Cook sausage in olive oil in large skillet until almost done. Stir frequently, so sausage browns on all sides.

2. Stir in bell pepper and onion. Cook 5 more minutes, stirring frequently.

3. Meanwhile, cook pasta in large pot of boiling water according to package directions.

4. Add broccoli during last 5 minutes of pasta's cooking time.

5. When pasta and broccoli are finished cooking, reserve ½ cup pasta cooking water. Drain remaining cooking water off pasta and broccoli. Keep pasta and broccoli warm.

6. To sausage mixture, add reserved cooking water, tomato, vinegar, and pepper flakes.

7. Place pasta and broccoli in large serving bowl. Toss with Parmesan cheese.

8. Top pasta and broccoli with sausage mixture and serve immediately.

Stuffed Pig Stomach

Michael L. Ervin
CENTRAL MARKET MANAGER

Makes 6–8 servings
Prep. Time: 30 minutes *Baking Time: 2–3 hours*

1 cleaned pig stomach

2–2½ lbs. loose fresh sausage

2 lbs. potatoes, diced

1 medium onion, minced

half a small head of cabbage, shredded

⅔ cup peeled carrots, shredded

¾ tsp. salt

¼–½ tsp. pepper

NOTE

If you're wary about this traditional Lancaster County dish, you don't have to eat the stomach itself. The stuffing, which has been flavored by the stomach, is great alone. Ketchup is a tasty condiment to eat on pig stomach.

1. Check interior of pig stomach to make sure it's clean.

2. Using cooking twine and skewers, sew shut any holes except the large one.

3. In a large bowl mix together all other ingredients.

4. Stuff loosely into stomach. (The stomach will shrink as it bakes.)

5. Sew opening shut with cooking twine and skewers.

6. Place stuffed stomach on a rack in a large roaster. Pour in enough water to cover bottom of roaster.

7. Bake covered 2–3 hours, or until stomach is beautifully browned.

8. Remove from pan and slice.

Country Meadows Lamburger

ORGANIC ACRES

Prep. Time: 5 minutes
Prep Time: 5 minutes ❧ Standing Time: 30 minutes ❧ Grilling Time: 15–20 minutes

1 lb. ground grass-fed lamb

1 Tbsp. fresh mint, *or* 1 tsp. dried mint, finely chopped

1 Tbsp. fresh oregano, *or* ½ tsp. dried oregano, finely chopped

½ tsp. salt

1. Mix all ingredients together.

2. Let stand for at least 30 minutes to let flavors blend.

3. Shape into 4 patties.

4. Grill 15–20 minutes, turning as needed, until cooked through to your liking.

Lamb Kabobs

Omar Saif
SAIF'S MIDDLE EASTERN FOODS

Makes 6-8 servings
Prep Time: 20 minutes ❧ Cooking Time: 20 minutes

4 slices bread, crusts removed and bread cubed

4–5 Tbsp. water

1 garlic clove, crushed

2 lbs. ground lamb

2 small onions, grated

¼ cup ground cumin

½ tsp. cayenne pepper

3 tsp. parsley, finely chopped

1 egg

½–¾ tsp. salt

¼–½ tsp. pepper

lemon wedges

1. Place bread cubes in a small bowl.

2. Add water slowly, just enough to dampen bread.

3. Add garlic. Squeeze garlic, bread, and water with your hands. Let stand 10 minutes.

4. While bread mixture is resting, combine ground lamb, grated onions, cumin, cayenne, and parsley together in a large bowl. Mix thoroughly by hand.

5. Knead in bread paste, egg, salt, and pepper. Mix by hand until all liquid is absorbed.

6. Roll meat mixture into 6"-8" long cylinders.

7. Pass skewer through the length of each cylinder. Pat meat mixture around skewer to secure it.

8. Cook kabobs over gray ash coals for about 20 minutes.

9. Rotate skewers occasionally until brown on all sides.

10. Serve with lemon wedges.

Grilled Leg of Lamb

Sam Neff
S. CLYDE WEAVER, INC.

Makes 8 servings
Prep. Time: 5 minutes 🌾 Marinating Time: 2 hours 🌾 Grilling Time: 30–45 minutes

5–6-lb. leg of lamb, boned
and butterflied

Marinade Ingredients:
¼ cup olive oil
1 Tbsp. oregano
1 tsp. rosemary
1 tsp. thyme
¼ tsp. black pepper

Final Basting Ingredients:
¼ cup lemon juice
½ tsp. oregano
1 tsp. salt

1. Mix all ingredients for oil marinade. Place butterflied leg in baking dish and pour marinade over top. Marinate 2 hours, turning occasionally.

2. Place leg on charcoal grill (gas grill tends to flame and needs water to control).

3. Use marinade oil to baste leg as it cooks, turning occasionally. Salt as you prefer.

4. Grill until thermometer registers 140° in thickest meat portion, about 20–30 minutes.

5. Mix final basting ingredients and use to baste leg. Continue grilling until thermometer registers 160° for pink and 175° for well done, about 10–15 more minutes.

6. Serve with lemon wedges.

NOTE

The lemon is used to cut the fat of the lamb. If you have ever been offended by the "wooliness" of lamb/mutton, this recipe is worth a try. The lemon makes a lot of difference. Do not use lemon baste too early in grilling process or it will dry out the meat.

Spiced Meatballs with White Raisins

Omar Saif

SAIF'S MIDDLE EASTERN FOODS

Makes 30 meatballs, or about 5–6 servings   ❦   *Prep Time: 20–30 minutes*
Standing/Chilling Time: 40 minutes   ❦   *Cooking Time: 6 minutes per skillet-full*

1 cup fresh white bread crumbs
½ cup plain yogurt
⅓ cup white raisins
boiling water
3 Tbsp. olive oil, *divided*
½ cup pine nuts
3 Tbsp. finely chopped scallions
1 clove garlic, finely chopped
1 tsp. cinnamon
1 tsp. ground allspice
1 tsp. salt
1 lb. ground lamb, *or beef, or* chicken
¼ tsp. hot pepper sauce

1. In a large mixing bowl, mix together bread crumbs and yogurt. Let soak about 10 minutes.

2. Place raisins in small bowl. Cover with boiling water. Allow to stand 10 minutes.

3. Meanwhile, heat 1 Tbsp. oil in skillet. Sauté pine nuts until golden. Drain and add to bread-yogurt mix.

4. Drain raisins. Stir into bread-yogurt mix.

5. Add scallions, garlic, cinnamon, allspice, and salt to bread-yogurt mixture. Stir together well.

6. Add meat. Using your hands, combine mixture thoroughly.

7. Heat remaining oil in large skillet. Form meat into small meatballs. Brown in batches in skillet, being careful not to crowd the pan. If you do, meatballs will steam and not brown.

8. Sauté meatballs for about 6 minutes per batch, turning to brown on all sides.

9. As meatballs finish, remove from skillet and keep warm. Serve with cooked rice.

Stuffed Flounder in Creamed Basil Sauce

Ethel Stoner
STONER'S VEGETABLES

Makes 6–8 servings
Prep. Time: 5 minutes ❦ *Cooking Time: 10 minutes* ❦ *Baking Time: 35 minutes*

¼ cup onion, chopped
4 Tbsp. butter *or* margarine
½ lb. fresh crabmeat *or* 7½-oz. can crabmeat
½ cup fresh mushrooms *or* 3-oz. can mushrooms, drained
½ cup cracker crumbs
2 Tbsp. parsley
2 Tbsp. mayonnaise
2 lbs. flounder fillets (8)
3 Tbsp. flour
1 cup milk
3-oz. pkg. cream cheese, softened
1 Tbsp. basil
dash of garlic powder
1 Tbsp. Worcestershire sauce
4 oz. Swiss cheese, grated
sprinkle of paprika

1. Sauté onion in 1 Tbsp. butter until onion is transparent. Stir in crabmeat, mushrooms, cracker crumbs, parsley and mayonnaise. Spread mixture over fillets.

2. Roll up fillets and place seam side down in greased baking dish.

3. Melt remaining 3 Tbsp. butter in saucepan. Blend in flour and add milk, cream cheese, and mushroom liquid (if desired). Cook mixture until it thickens. Add basil, garlic powder and Worcestershire sauce.

4. Pour mixture over fillets in baking dish. Bake at 400° for 25 minutes. Remove from oven and sprinkle with Swiss cheese and paprika. Return to oven and bake 10 minutes longer.

Salmon Cakes with Spicy Mayo

Thelma Thomas
SPRING GLEN

Makes 4 servings
Prep. Time: 20 minutes ❧ Cooking Time: 10–12 minutes

2 large salmon fillets, cooked, *or*
2 15½-oz. cans salmon, drained and deboned

2 eggs, beaten

¾ cup bread crumbs, *divided*

½ cup red bell pepper, minced

¼ cup red, *or* green, onions, minced

1 tsp. minced garlic

2 tsp. Old Bay seasoning

freshly ground pepper

2 Tbsp. fresh chives, chopped

1 Tbsp. fresh dill, chopped

1 tsp. Tabasco sauce

zest and juice from 1 lemon

1 Tbsp. olive oil

Spicy Mayo Sauce:
½ cup mayonnaise

2 Tbsp. medium salsa

few dashes of Tabasco sauce

2 tsp. dill-pickle relish

1. In a good-sized mixing bowl, mix together salmon, eggs, ½ cup bread crumbs, peppers, onions, garlic, seasonings, zest, and juice.

2. Form mixture into 8 Salmon Cakes.

3. In a small bowl, mix ¼ cup reserved bread crumbs with 1 Tbsp. olive oil.

4. Place Salmon Cakes on a greased baking sheet.

5. Sprinkle with oiled bread crumbs.

6. Bake at 400° for 10–12 minutes, or until lightly browned.

7. Mix Sauce ingredients together. Serve with baked Salmon Cakes.

Crab Cakes with Cajun Mayonnaise

Christine Hess
WENDY JO'S HOMEMADE

Makes 6-8 servings
Prep. Time: 20 minutes 🌱 Cooking Time: 10 minutes

Red Cajun Mayonnaise Sauce:

1 red bell pepper (blackened slightly)

1 dill pickle spear, sliced

2 chopped green onions

1 jalapeño pepper (no seeds)

2 Tbsp. chopped parsley

2 cups mayonnaise

½ tsp. hot sauce

1 tsp. lemon zest

Crab Cakes:

1 lb. back fin crabmeat

1 lb. lump crabmeat

2 eggs, slightly beaten

2 tsp. Worcestershire sauce

2 tsp. dry mustard

1½–2 cups Italian bread crumbs

olive oil

1. To make Sauce, mix bell pepper, pickle, onions, jalapeño pepper, parsley, mayonnaise, hot sauce, and lemon zest in food processor or blender. Blend until smooth.

2. Refrigerate until serving.

3. Remove all loose shells from crabmeat and place meat in mixing bowl.

4. Add eggs, Worcestershire sauce, mustard, and bread crumbs.

5. If mixture is too dry, add a little more mayonnaise.

6. Shape into 8–10 Crab Cakes. Sauté in skillet with a dash of olive oil to prevent sticking.

7. Sauté 3–4 minutes per side, until golden brown.

TIPS

1. *Serve Mayo Sauce in a small bowl or use a pastry bag and swirl a zig-zag on plate before placing Crab Cakes on top of it.*

2. *Place a lemon wedge by each serving for garnish/flavoring.*

Crabmeat au Gratin

Rose Meck
MECK'S PRODUCE

Makes 6 servings
Prep. Time: 20 minutes ❦ Baking Time: 20 minutes

half a stick (4 Tbsp.) butter
¼ cup flour
1 cup heavy, or whipping, cream
1 cup milk
1 tsp. Worcestershire sauce
½ tsp. salt
¼ tsp. ground black pepper
2 Tbsp. finely diced celery
1 Tbsp. grated onion
1 Tbsp. chopped pimiento
¾ cup shredded sharp cheddar cheese, *divided*
1 lb. lump crabmeat, picked over to remove shell fragments

1. Preheat oven to 350°. Butter a 6-cup baking dish.

2. In saucepan, melt butter over medium heat.

3. Whisk in flour and cook, stirring constantly, for 2-3 minutes. Be careful not to brown the flour.

4. Remove from heat and slowly whisk in cream and milk.

5. Stir in Worcestershire sauce, salt, pepper, celery, onion, and pimiento.

6. Add ½ cup cheese and the crabmeat. Mix well.

7. Spoon mixture into casserole and top with remaining ¼ cup cheese.

8. Bake approximately 20 minutes, or until cheese is lightly browned.

9. Serve at once.

When one takes the time to care about people, great recipes are shared across a market stand.

Also, a customer friend, Pam, and I share a love for orchids. She takes care of a special orchid for me. When it blooms, she returns it to me. When it's finished blooming, I return it to her.

— ROSE MECK, Meck's Produce

Lemon Shrimp and Pasta

Cindy Cover
PLUM STREET GOURMET

Makes 4 servings

Prep. Time: 45 minutes ❦ Marinating Time 3¾ hours ❦ Cooking Time: 20 minutes

2 Tbsp. olive oil

4 garlic cloves, crushed, *divided*

1 Tbsp. fresh thyme, chopped

zest of 1 lemon

juice of 2 lemons

ground black pepper

20 jumbo shrimp, peeled and de-veined, with tails on

2 Tbsp. olive oil

1 Tbsp. butter

the white part of 2 large leeks, thoroughly washed and cut into julienne strips

2 tomatoes, seeded and chopped

juice of 1 lemon

8–12 ozs. pasta, cooked and drained

1. Mix together 2 Tbsp. olive oil, 2 garlic cloves, thyme, lemon zest, juice of 2 lemons and pepper.

2. Marinate shrimp in refrigerator in this mixture for 3 hours; then marinate at room temperature for 45 minutes.

3. In a skillet over medium heat, melt together 2 Tbsp. olive oil, 1 Tbsp. butter, and remaining 2 cloves crushed garlic. Add leeks. Cook on low heat, stirring often until leeks are caramelized.

4. Stir in tomatoes and heat briefly. Increase heat to a high setting.

5. Add shrimp and marinade. Sauté quickly, just until shrimp turn opaque. Remove from heat.

6. Add juice of one lemon. Toss with hot pasta. Serve immediately.

Summer Garden Pasta Sauce

Connie Butto
THE HERB SHOP

Makes 4–6 servings
Prep. Time: 20–25 minutes ❦ Cooking Time: 7 minutes ❦ Standing/Chilling Time: 8 hours, or overnight

1½–2 lbs. fresh plum tomatoes, coarsely chopped
1 medium onion, chopped
10 green *or* black olives, chopped
½ cup fresh parsley, minced
3 Tbsp. fresh basil, minced
4 tsp. capers
½ tsp. paprika
½ tsp. dried oregano
1¼ Tbsp. red wine vinegar
½ cup olive oil
1 lb. cooked pasta, preferably tomato-basil fettucini

1. In a large bowl, mix tomatoes, onion, olives, parsley, basil, capers, paprika, and oregano together. Add vinegar and oil. Mix. Cover. Refrigerate overnight.

2. One hour before serving, allow mixture to come to room temperature.

3. Cook pasta. Combine pasta with other ingredients and serve.

Scallops and Pasta Romano

Cynthia Strube
MARION CHEESE

Makes 6 servings
Prep. Time: 25–30 minutes ❦ Cooking Time: 15–20 minutes

1 lb. bay scallops
2 cloves garlic, minced
half a stick (4 Tbsp.) butter
half a stick (4 Tbsp.) butter, softened
2 Tbsp. dried parsley flakes

1. In a large skillet, cook scallops and garlic in half a stick butter (which has not been softened) until scallops are done. Keep warm.

2. In a large bowl, combine softened butter, parsley, and basil. Blend in pepper and cream

¼ tsp. dried basil

¼ tsp. black pepper

8-oz. pkg. cream cheese, softened

⅔ cup boiling water

8 ozs. fettuccini, linguine, *or* spaghetti

¾ cup Romano *or* Parmesan cheese, grated, *divided*

NOTE

This is a wonderful combination of seafood, pasta, and spices!

cheese. Stir in boiling water and mix well. Keep warm over pan of hot water.

3. Cook pasta according to package directions and drain.

4. Toss scallop mixture into pasta. Sprinkle with ½ cup grated cheese and toss.

5. Pour cream cheese mixture over pasta and toss until well coated. Place pasta into serving dish and sprinkle with remaining ¼ cup grated cheese.

Penné Bosciaola

Janelle and Kendal Yoder
LETTUCE TOSS SALAD

Makes 4-6 servings
Prep. Time: 15 minutes ❦ Cooking Time: 20 minutes

half a red onion, sliced

2 cloves garlic, finely chopped

¾ stick (6 Tbsp.) butter, *divided*

5 ozs. shiitake mushrooms, sliced

2 pints cherry tomatoes, cut in half

½–¾ tsp. salt

¼ tsp. freshly ground pepper

¾ cup chicken broth, *or* vegetable broth

2–3 handfuls arugula, *or* fresh spinach

¾ cup fresh basil, chopped

4 ozs. Romano cheese, grated

12 ozs. penne pasta, cooked, drained, and kept warm.

1. In large skillet, lightly sauté onion and garlic in 2 Tbsp. butter until translucent.

2. Add mushrooms. Cook 1 minute.

3. Add cherry tomatoes, salt and pepper. Cook 30 seconds.

4. Finish by stirring in broth, arugula, basil, remaining butter cut in chunks, and cheese.

5. Stir just until heated through.

6. Toss with cooked pasta.

NOTE

We enjoy whole wheat pasta with this recipe.

Orecchiette with Olives, Vegetables, and Mozzarella

Regine Ibold
REGINE'S COFFEE

Makes 4 servings

Prep. Time: 20 minutes ❧ Cooking Time: 10 minutes ❧ Baking Time: 10–12 minutes

3 Tbsp. olive oil

2 medium zucchini, washed and cut into ½" cubes

½ tsp. salt

½ tsp. freshly ground pepper

8 ozs. orecchiette pasta

1 Tbsp. salt

1 cup black olives, pitted and chopped

4 ripe plum tomatoes, halved and diced

1 cup Parmesan cheese, grated, *divided*

freshly ground pepper

8 ozs. fresh mozzarella, cut in ½" cubes

1. In a good-sized skillet, sauté zucchini in oil over medium heat for about 5 minutes.

2. Stir in ½ tsp. salt and pepper. Drain zucchini into a large bowl.

3. Cook pasta in water with 1 Tbsp. salt, for about 10 minutes. Drain well.

4. Mix pasta and zucchini together.

5. Set oven to 375°. Grease a 9" × 13" baking dish.

6. Stir olives, tomatoes, and ½ cup Parmesan cheese into zucchini-pasta mixture. Add freshly ground pepper to taste.

7. Spoon into baking dish and sprinkle with mozzarella cheese cubes.

8. Bake 10–12 minutes, or until cheese is melted.

9. Serve with remaining Parmesan cheese.

Parsley Pasta

Sara Neilon
CENTRAL MARKET CUSTOMER

Makes 6 servings
Prep. Time: 20 minutes   Cooking Time: 20–30 minutes

1 lb. angel hair pasta, *or any other favorite pasta*

⅓ cup olive oil, *divided*

1 large onion, finely chopped

1 red bell pepper, cut in long strips

1–2 cloves garlic, minced

1 large bunch parsley

½ tsp. salt

¼ tsp. pepper

1–2 Tbsp. freshly squeezed lemon juice

¼–½ tsp. red pepper flakes, *optional*

1½ cups Parmesan cheese, shredded, *divided*

1. Prepare pasta according to package directions. Drain and keep warm.

2. Meanwhile, finely chop onion. Sauté in 2 Tbsp. olive oil in large skillet until golden, about 8–10 minutes.

3. Stir red pepper strips into skillet halfway through onion cooking time.

4. Stir garlic into skillet just at end of onion cooking time. Turn off heat, but keep contents warm.

5. Chop parsley very fine.

6. In a medium-sized bowl, combine parsley, remaining olive oil, salt, pepper, lemon juice, and red pepper flakes if you wish.

7. Stir into cooked pasta.

8. Stir in 1 cup Parmesan, coating pasta evenly.

9. Serve with additional Parmesan cheese sprinkled on top.

NOTE

This is a very flexible recipe, and a great way to use a large quantity of parsley.

Whole Wheat Ricotta Gnocchi with Swiss Chard

Betsey Sterenfeld
CENTRAL MARKET CUSTOMER

Makes 8-10 servings ❧ *Prep. Time: 30 minutes* ❧ *Cooking Time: 25 minutes*

Gnocchi:

2 cups whole milk ricotta

2 large eggs, lightly beaten

1½ cups Parmesan cheese, *divided*

¼ tsp. nutmeg, grated

¼ tsp. salt

¼ tsp. pepper

1⅜ cups whole wheat pastry flour

Sauce:

3 lbs. Swiss chard

4 cloves garlic

2 Tbsp. olive oil

½ lbs. ham, *or* bacon, roughly chopped

salt

red pepper flakes

Parmigiano-Reggiano

1. Prepare Swiss chard by removing leaves from stems. Chop stems into ¼"–½" slices. Tear leaves into bite-sized pieces. Set stems and leaves aside.

2. To make Gnocchi, stir together ricotta, eggs, 1 cup Parmesan, nutmeg, salt, and pepper in large mixing bowl.

3. Add flour. Stir to form a soft, wet dough.

4. Divide dough in half. With lightly floured hands, roll each half on a well-floured work surface into a 1"-diameter rope.

5. Cut dough ropes into 1"-thick pieces. Make a small indentation in center of each piece.

6. Set formed Gnocchi in a single layer on floured, parchment-lined baking sheets, without touching each other.

7. While forming dough, bring large pot of salted water to boil.

8. Cook half the Gnocchi in boiling water until all have all risen to the surface, about 3–4 minutes.

9. Scoop Gnocchi into colander with slotted spoon.

10 Repeat with second batch of Gnocchi.

11. To make Sauce, sauté garlic cloves in olive oil in very large skillet (or Dutch oven) over medium heat.

One of my favorite Central Market moments is hearing Earl Groff (of Groff's Produce) talk about life's cycles and the challenges inherent in growing his beautiful rainbow chard. He's inspired me to find new ways to cook all of the beloved veggies I find at his stand.
— BETSEY STERENFELD, Central Market customer

12. Remove garlic when cloves are aromatic and a light brown color. Discard cloves.

13. Add ham or bacon to flavored oil in skillet. Cook until crisp.

14. Add chopped chard stems. Lightly season with salt and red pepper flakes.

15. When stems begin to become tender, add chard leaves.

16. Cook until leaves wilt but are not mushy.

17. Transfer cooked gnocchi to skillet with chard.

18. Sprinkle with remaining cheese and toss.

19. Serve immediately.

Luscious Lancaster Tomatoes, Pasta-Filled

Pat Golden
CENTRAL MARKET CUSTOMER

Makes 6 servings ❧ *Prep. Time: 35 minutes* ❧ *Cooking Time: 15 minutes*

6 large tomatoes
¼ lb. orzo
¼ cup fresh parsley, chopped
1 garlic clove, minced
¼ cup fresh basil, chopped, or ½ tsp. dried oregano
salt to taste
pepper to taste
¼ cup olive oil
¼ cup Parmesan, or Romano, cheese

1. Cut off tomato tops. Spoon out seeds and cut away pulp. Chop pulp finely.

2. Salt interior of tomatoes.

3. Turn tomatoes over and allow them to drain for about 30 minutes.

4. Cook pasta al dente and drain well.

5. Mix pasta with parsley, garlic, and basil or oregano. Add salt and pepper if needed. Spoon mixture into tomatoes. Drizzle with olive oil and cheese.

6. Lightly oil a baking dish just large enough to hold the tomatoes.

7. Bake for 15 minutes at 350°, or until tomatoes have softened slightly.

8. Serve hot or at room temperature.

Spinach and Tomato Omelet

Janelle Glick

LANCASTER GENERAL WELLNESS PARTNERSHIP

Makes 1 serving

Prep. Time: 5 minutes ❧ Cooking Time: about 5 minutes

1 tsp. extra-virgin olive oil

5 cherry tomatoes, halved

1 scallion, sliced

1 cup baby spinach, washed, but not completely dry

½ cup liquid egg substitute

¼ cup shredded reduced-fat cheddar cheese

⅛ tsp. salt

⅛ tsp. freshly ground pepper

1 Tbsp. water

1. Spray small nonstick skillet with cooking spray.

2. Add oil and place over medium-high heat.

3. When skillet is hot, add tomatoes and scallion. Cook, stirring once or twice, until vegetables soften, 1–2 minutes.

4. Place spinach on top of vegetables. Cover and let wilt, about 30 seconds. Stir to combine.

5. Pour in egg substitute. Reduce heat to medium-low and continue cooking, stirring constantly with a heatproof rubber spatula, until egg starts to set, about 20 seconds.

6. Continue cooking, lifting edges so uncooked egg flows underneath, until mostly set, about 30 seconds more.

7. Sprinkle cheese, salt, and pepper over omelet. Lift up an edge of the omelet and drizzle tablespoon of water under it.

8. Cover, reduce heat to low, and cook until egg is completely set and cheese is melted, about 2 minutes.

9. Fold over, using the spatula, and serve.

Tomato and Basil Pie

Rose Meck
MECK'S PRODUCE

Makes 4-8 servings
Prep. Time: 30 minutes ❧ *Baking Time: 45-50 minutes*

9" prepared pie crust, unbaked

1½ cups shredded mozzarella cheese, *divided*

5 plum, *or* 4 medium-sized, tomatoes

1 cup loosely-packed fresh basil leaves, plus additional leaves for garnish

4 cloves garlic

½ cup mayonnaise

¼ cup grated Parmesan cheese

⅛ tsp. ground white pepper

1. Preheat oven to 375°. Fill pie crust with raw rice or pie weights. Bake for 10 minutes.

2. Remove crust from oven and empty of weights. Sprinkle with ½ cup mozzarella cheese. Cool on wire rack.

3. Cut tomatoes into wedges. Drain on paper towels.

4. Arrange tomato wedges on top of melted cheese in baked pie shell.

5. In a food processor, combine basil and garlic, processing until coarsely chopped. Sprinkle over tomatoes.

6. In medium-sized mixing bowl, combine remaining mozzarella, mayonnaise, Parmesan, and pepper.

7. Spoon cheese mixture over basil mixture, spreading to cover evenly.

8. Bake 35–40 minutes, or until top is golden and bubbly.

9. Serve warm, garnished with basil leaves.

Corn Pie

Cynthia Strube
MARION CHEESE

Makes one 9" pie
Prep. Time: 10 minutes ❧ Baking Time: 45 minutes

9" double pie crust, unbaked
2 cups fresh corn
½ cup milk
1 Tbsp. butter
1 tsp. salt
1 tsp. sugar
1 Tbsp. parsley, chopped
2 hard-boiled eggs, diced

1. Line 9" pie pan with pie shell.

2. In a small saucepan, heat corn with milk and butter.

3. Remove from heat and carefully stir in remaining ingredients. Spoon corn mixture into pie pan.

4. Cover top with pastry. Prick top with fork.

5. Bake at 400° for 10 minutes. Reduce oven temperature to 325° and bake an additional 35 minutes. Serve hot.

Eggplant Parmesan

Rose Meck
MECK'S PRODUCE

Makes 6 servings
Prep. Time: 35 minutes ❧ Baking Time: 15 minutes

1 medium eggplant
1 Tbsp. cooking oil
1 cup bread crumbs
½ cup Parmesan cheese
2 Tbsp. parsley flakes
1 tsp. salt
1 tsp. dried oregano
6 small tomatoes, chopped

1. Peel eggplant. Cut into ½"-thick slices.

2. Brown lightly on both sides in large skillet in cooking oil. Place into a lightly greased 9" × 13" baking dish.

3. In a small bowl, mix together bread crumbs, cheese, parsley, salt, and oregano. Sprinkle mixture evenly over eggplant slices.

2 medium onions, chopped

1 green, *or* red, bell pepper, chopped

2 dashes garlic salt

2 Tbsp. oil

½ cup tomato sauce

1 cup cheddar cheese, grated

4. In a saucepan combine tomatoes, onions, peppers, garlic salt, oil, and tomato sauce. Simmer for 15 minutes.

5. Spoon over top of eggplant slices in baking dish. Top with grated cheddar cheese.

6. Bake at 375° for 15 minutes.

Eggplant Creole

Ethel Stoner
STONER'S VEGETABLES

Makes 4-6 servings
Prep. Time: 30 minutes   Baking Time: 30 minutes

1 medium eggplant

3 Tbsp. butter

3 Tbsp. flour

3 large tomatoes, *or* 2 cups canned tomatoes

1 small green pepper, chopped

1 small onion, chopped

1 tsp. salt

1 Tbsp. brown sugar

1 bay leaf

2 cloves

½–¾ cup bread crumbs

chunks of butter

1. Peel eggplant and dice into 1" squares. Simmer in about 1 inch of lightly salted water in a saucepan for 12 minutes.

2. Drain and place in greased 2-quart baking dish.

3. In saucepan melt butter. Add flour and stir until well blended.

4. If using fresh tomatoes, peel and chop. Add tomatoes, pepper, and onion to butter and flour mixture.

5. Add salt, brown sugar, bay leaf, and cloves. Cook 5–10 minutes.

6. Remove bay leaf and cloves. Pour mixture over eggplant in baking dish.

7. Cover with bread crumbs and dot with butter.

8. Bake at 350° for 30 minutes.

Vegetable Pizza

Anna Mary Glick
LETTUCE TOSS SALAD

Makes 8-10 servings

Prep. Time: 1 hour ❧ *Baking Time: 15-20 minutes* ❧ *Cooling Time: 20 minutes*

Crust:

half a stick (4 Tbsp.) butter

2 Tbsp. sugar

¼ cup boiling water

1 pkg. dry active yeast

¼ very warm water

1 small egg, beaten

1½ cups flour

1 tsp. salt

Toppings:

1 envelope dry ranch-style dressing

1 pint sour cream

½–1 cup carrots, shredded

½–1 cup celery, diced

½–1 cup green peppers diced

½–1 cup lettuce, shredded

½–1 cup cheese, shredded

½–1 cup broccoli, cut fine

½–1 cup cauliflower, cut fine

1. In a large bowl combine butter, sugar, and boiling water. Stir until sugar is dissolved.

2. In a small bowl sprinkle yeast into very warm water. Let stand a few minutes; then stir to dissolve.

3. Add beaten egg to yeast mixture.

4. Add contents of small bowl to large bowl. Add flour and salt. Mix well.

5. Allow to cool.

6. Transfer to a well-greased baking pan with sides. Grease your fingers well. Press dough evenly into bottom and corners of pan.

7. Bake at 325° until golden brown.

8. While crust is baking, mix dressing into sour cream. Refrigerate until needed.

9. Allow crust to cool thoroughly.

10. Spread with flavored sour cream. Sprinkle evenly with toppings.

11. Cut into slices and serve immediately.

Zucchini Pizza Casserole

Katie Ann Stoltzfus

Makes 6 servings
Prep. Time: 20 minutes & Cooking Time: 60 minutes

4 eggs
½ cup vegetable oil
1 cup flour
¼ tsp. baking powder
½ tsp. garlic powder
1 tsp. salt
3 cups grated zucchini, unpeeled
1 onion, chopped
2 cups pizza sauce, *or* salsa
1–1½ cups grated mozzarella, *or* cheddar, cheese

1. Beat eggs in large mixing bowl. Stir in oil, flour, baking powder, garlic powder, and salt.

2. Stir in zucchini and onion and mix well.

3. Pour into 9" square greased baking dish.

4. Bake 45 minutes.

5. Remove from oven and cover with pizza sauce or salsa. Sprinkle cheese over top.

6. Return to oven and bake 15 minutes longer.

VARIATION

If you wish, add your choice of pizza toppings in Step 5, after covering the pizza with sauce and before sprinkling with cheese. Sliced black olives and fresh basil are good. As a departure from a vegetarian dish, you can also add cooked hamburger, chicken, or sausage.

Dutch Noodles Florentine

Mary Ellen Campbell
BASKETS OF CENTRAL MARKET

Makes 6 servings
Prep. Time: 10 minutes ❧ Cooking Time: 40–50 minutes

1 lb. bacon

1 lb. noodles, variety of your choosing

1 lb. fresh spinach, *or* 10-oz. pkg. frozen spinach

1 stick (8 Tbsp.) butter

1 egg, slightly beaten

1½ cups heavy cream

2 cups Parmesan cheese, freshly grated

salt and pepper to taste

1. In a large skillet, cook bacon until crisp. Drain it. Crumble and set aside.

2. In a large saucepan, cook noodles according to directions. Drain and set aside.

3. If using fresh spinach, wash well and drain. If using frozen spinach, thaw and squeeze dry.

4. Melt butter in large heavy saucepan. Add spinach and heat through.

5. Add drained noodles and toss lightly with spinach.

6. In another pan, combine egg, cream, cheese, salt, and pepper. Heat over very low heat for 5 minutes.

7. Pour cream sauce over spinach-noodle mixture. Toss together gently.

8. Serve in a heated dish.

BREAKFASTS

Country Breakfast

Rebecca Lapp
LAPP'S DELI

Christine Hess
WENDY JO'S HOMEMADE

Makes 10–12 servings ❦ *Prep. Time: 15 minutes*
Chilling Time: overnight, or 8 hours ❦ *Cooking Time: 1 hour* ❦ *Standing Time: 15 minutes*

14–16 slices bread (enough to fill your 9" × 13" baking pan), *divided*

1 lb. fully cooked chipped *or* cubed ham, *divided*

1 lb. cheddar cheese, shredded, *divided*

1 lb. mozzarella cheese, shredded, *divided*

6 eggs

3 cups milk

½ tsp. dry mustard

1 stick (8 Tbsp.) butter

2–3 cups lightly crushed cornflakes

1. Lightly grease a 9" × 13" baking pan.

2. Layer in half the bread, ham, and cheese.

3. Repeat to make a second layer.

4. Beat eggs in a good-sized mixing bowl. Stir in milk and dry mustard.

5. Pour over layers.

6. Melt butter. Toss butter and cornflakes in a bowl.

7. Spoon buttered cornflakes over top of layers just before baking.

8. Cover and refrigerate overnight.

9. Uncover and bake at 375° for one hour. Allow to stand 15 minutes before serving.

Scrambled Eggs with Celery and Onions

Trish Hillegas
SWEETHEARTS OF LANCASTER COUNTY

Makes 4 servings
Prep. Time: 15 minutes ✽ Cooking Time: 10 minutes

3 Tbsp. butter
1½ cups finely chopped onions
¼ cup finely chopped celery
½ tsp. salt
¼ tsp. pepper
12 eggs, beaten
1 Tbsp. fresh, *or* 1 tsp. dried, parsley

1. In a large skillet, cook butter, onions, celery, salt, and pepper together for 3 minutes, stirring constantly.

2. Add beaten eggs and scramble together with cooked vegetables and seasoning.

3. Fold in parsley and serve immediately.

THE CENTRAL MARKET, A CITY EDIFICE TO BE PROUD OF

A fine example of the Romanesque Style of Architecture
which Reflects Credit on the Architect and Contractor.
Good Accommodations

The lighting of the building is partly obtained from numerous large windows on all sides, raised above the side stalls, but mainly from small dormer windows on all sides scattered all about the roof, the effect of this arrangement being very pleasing. The floor, which has a general, easy slope from east to west, is of concrete and is admirably adapted to secure cleanliness, as it can easily be flushed with water from plugs placed at convenient points. This fine even floor, so easily cleaned will leave no excuse for a dirty, ill smelling market, a subject of much universal complaint ... The architect has confined himself principally to the south front in the design, and expenditure for ornament, as most of the other parts of the building are so surrounded by buildings as not to be much seen. This elevation shows a tower upon each corner and a gable in the centre ...

— *THE NEW ERA*, Lancaster, Saturday, October 5, 1889

Sausage and Peach Bake

Rose Rohrer
ROHRER'S FLOWERS

Makes 12 servings

Prep. Time: 10 minutes ❧ *Cooking Time: 20 minutes* ❧ *Baking Time: 25 minutes*

2 cups pancake mix

16-oz. can peach slices, drained, juice reserved

½ lb. sausage links

Peach Syrup:

¼ cup sugar

1 Tbsp. cornstarch

¾ cup maple-flavored syrup

1 Tbsp. butter

1. Prepare pancake mix according to directions *except* use only 1 cup liquid in place of amount called for in directions.

2. Pour into greased 9" × 13" baking pan.

3. Cut each sausage link in half lengthwise. Brown in skillet.

4. Arrange sausages and peach slices on top of batter.

5. Bake at 350° for 25 minutes, or until toothpick inserted in center comes out clean.

6. While mix is baking, prepare Peach Syrup by combining sugar and cornstarch in a small saucepan.

7. Stir in reserved peach juice. Cook, stirring until syrup is thickened and smooth.

8. Stir in maple-flavored syrup and butter until butter is melted.

9. Serve hot, accompanied with warm Peach Syrup.

TIP

You can fully prepare this recipe the night before serving it, and then reheat it in the morning. Or do everything but bake the recipe the night before, refrigerate it overnight, and bake it the next morning.

Overnight Sausage Soufflé

Jean Styles
KIEFER MEATS

Makes 6 servings
Prep. Time: 20 minutes ❧ Chilling Time: overnight, or 8 hours ❧ Baking Time: 45 minutes

1 lb. sausage, links *or* loose

6 slices white bread, cubed

1½ cups shredded cheddar cheese

4 eggs

1½ cups milk

¼–½ tsp. salt, according to your taste preference

1. One day before serving, brown sausage and drain. (If you're using links, cut each into thirds.)

2. Layer bread, sausage, and cheese in a lightly greased 2½-quart deep baking dish.

3. In a mixing bowl, combine eggs, milk, and salt.

4. Pour over layers.

5. Cover and refrigerate overnight.

6. Next day, bake at 325° for 45 minutes.

NOTE

This is a special and substantial breakfast for anytime. It is our traditional Christmas-morning breakfast, along with fresh fruit salad and sticky buns.

French Toast Casserole

Sally Delgiorno

DELGIORNO'S ITALIAN SPECIALTIES

Makes 6–8 servings ❧ *Prep. Time: 15 minutes*
Chilling Time: 4–36 hours ❧ *Baking Time: 45–50 minutes* ❧ *Standing Time: 5 minutes*

10-oz. French baguette *or*
Italian bread

8 large eggs

3 cups milk

4 tsp. sugar

¾ tsp. salt

1 Tbsp. vanilla

2 Tbsp. butter, cut into small pieces

1. Cut bread into 1" slices and arrange on bottom of greased 9" × 13" baking pan.

2. In a good-sized mixing bowl, beat eggs. Add milk, sugar, salt, and vanilla, mixing till well blended.

3. Pour over bread.

4. Cover with foil and refrigerate 4–36 hours.

5. When ready to bake, uncover and dot with butter.

6. Bake, uncovered, at 350° for 45–50 minutes, or until puffy and lightly browned.

7. Let stand 5 minutes.

8. Serve with syrup, honey, yogurt, sour cream, and/or fresh fruit.

Banana Coffee Cake

Wendy Hess
WENDY JO'S HOMEMADE

Makes 6-9 servings
Prep. Time: 20 minutes ❧ Cooking Time: 40-50 minutes

Cake:

1 stick (½ cup) butter, softened
¾ cup sugar
1 egg
3 Tbsp. buttermilk
1⅓ cups mashed, ripe bananas
1½ cups flour
¾ tsp. baking soda
¾ tsp. baking powder
½ tsp. salt

Streusel:

1 cup semi-sweet chocolate chips
½ cup, plus 2 Tbsp., brown sugar
½ cup chopped walnuts
1 Tbsp. cinnamon

1. Using an electric mixer, cream together butter and sugar.

2. Mix in egg, buttermilk, and bananas until thoroughly combined.

3. In a separate bowl, combine flour, baking soda, baking powder, and salt.

4. Stir into wet ingredients until just blended.

5. Spread half of cake mixture into greased 8" × 8" baking pan.

6. In a separate bowl, stir Streusel ingredients together. Sprinkle half of Streusel evenly over top.

7. Carefully spoon remaining cake batter on top. Spread out, but without disturbing the Streusel crumbs.

8. Sprinkle remaining Streusel over top.

9. Bake at 350° for 40 minutes, or until toothpick inserted in center comes out clean.

 Tuesday mornings on Market find me scoping out which produce stand has the ripest bananas!

— WENDY HESS, Wendy Jo's Homemade

BREADS

Homemade White Bread

Rachel Stoltzfus
STOLTZFUS BAKED GOODS

Makes 2 loaves

Prep. Time: 20–25 minutes ❧ *Rising Time: about 3 hours* ❧ *Baking Time: 25 minutes*

1½ Tbsp. yeast

1 Tbsp. sugar

2 cups warm water, *divided*

½ cup cooking oil

⅓ cup sugar

1 Tbsp. salt

5½ cups occident, *or* white bread, flour

1. In a 2-cup glass measuring cup, sprinkle yeast and 1 Tbsp. sugar into 1 cup warm water. Let stand 10 minutes.

2. Pour yeast mixture into large mixing bowl. Gradually add oil, remaining 1 cup warm water, ⅓ cup sugar, salt, and flour, stirring constantly.

3. When well mixed, pour dough onto lightly floured board. Knead well, until dough is no longer sticky.

4. Cover with a tea towel. Let rise in a warm place. Check after 1 hour; dough should have doubled in size.

5. Punch down. Cover and let rise another hour.

6. Punch down. Divide dough in half. Shape into two loaves. Put into two greased loaf pans. Pierce tops with fork.

7. Let rise until dough comes a little above tops of pans, about 30–60 minutes.

8. Bake at 350° for 25 minutes.

9. Remove from pans and let cool on a wire rack.

Tiny Cream Cheese Biscuits

Susan Stoeckl
SUSAN'S SECRET GARDEN

Makes 24 mini-muffins
Prep. Time: 10 minutes ❧ Baking Time: 15–17 minutes

8-oz. pkg. cream cheese, softened
1 stick (8 Tbsp.) butter, softened
1 cup self-rising flour

VARIATION

You can add fresh herbs, some grated cheese, or bits of bacon to these muffins. Gently fold the extra ingredients into the batter between Steps 2 and 3.

1. With electric mixer, beat cream cheese and butter at medium speed till creamy, approximately two minutes.

2. Gradually add flour, beating at low speed just until blended.

3. Spoon dough into ungreased mini-muffin pans, filling full.

4. Bake at 400° for 15–17 minutes, or until golden.

5. Serve warm.

 Many years ago, why was it acceptable for women to work on market? I think there were several reasons. First of all, it was only a part-time job. I would have felt badly about hiring a mother of young children to work full-time. Also, many mothers took their children along to market. My mother took me when I was only six weeks old.
— ANNA MARY NEFF, S. Clyde Weaver, Inc.

Delicious Cornbread

Janelle and Kendal Yoder
LETTUCE TOSS SALAD

Makes 9 servings
Prep. Time: 10 minutes   Baking Time: 18-20 minutes

2 tsp. baking powder
1 cup yellow cornmeal
1 cup flour
½ tsp. baking soda
1 egg
1 cup buttermilk
¼ cup honey
3 Tbsp. butter, melted

1. Mix dry ingredients together in a good-sized mixing bowl.

2. Beat together egg, buttermilk, and honey in a medium-sized bowl.

3. Add wet ingredients to dry ingredients. Mix together gently until fully combined.

4. Stir in melted butter.

5. Pour batter into greased 8" square baking pan.

6. Bake at 425° for 18–20 minutes, or until toothpick inserted in center of bread comes out clean.

VARIATION

If you don't have buttermilk, use this tip from my grandmother: Place 1 Tbsp. lemon juice or vinegar into a 1-cup measure. Fill the cup with milk. Stir and let stand for 2 minutes. Then use in place of buttermilk in a recipe.

Light-as-a-Feather Cornbread

Becky Friedrich
THOMAS PRODUCE

Makes 16 servings
Prep. Time: 15 minutes ❧ Baking Time: 20 minutes

¾ cup all-purpose flour
¾ cup rye flour
½ cup cornmeal
3 tsp. baking powder
2 eggs
½ cup sugar
1 stick (8 Tbsp.) butter, melted
1 cup whole milk, warm

1. Mix dry ingredients together in a good-sized mixing bowl.

2. Mix eggs, sugar, and melted butter in another good-sized bowl.

3. Mix dry ingredients alternately with milk into egg mixture.

4. Pour into greased 9" square baking pan.

5. Bake at 425° for about 20 minutes, or until toothpick inserted in center of bread comes out clean.

As a boy, I went to Market early in the morning around 4 a.m. to help set up Dad's meat stand. Then around 6:30 a.m., my grandfather Elmer Thomas would take me down to the Queen Street Restaurant and buy me breakfast—two glazed doughnuts and a cup of hot chocolate. What a treat! This was the only time I got glazed doughnuts. That made getting up at 3:30 a.m. worth it.
— ERNIE THOMAS, C. H. Thomas and Sons

Banana Bread

Janelle and Kendal Yoder
LETTUCE TOSS SALAD

Makes 1 loaf
Prep. Time: 15-20 minutes ❦ *Baking Time: 70-75 minutes*

2 cups unbleached flour

¾ cup sugar

1 tsp. baking soda

½ tsp. salt

1 tsp. cinnamon

¼ tsp. ground allspice

¼ tsp. ground nutmeg

1 cup coarsely chopped walnuts
or pecans, *optional*

¾–1 cup chocolate chips, *optional*

3 large, very ripe, well mashed
bananas, about 1½ cups

½ cup vanilla, *or* plain, yogurt
(you can also use ¼ cup
applesauce and ¼ cup yogurt)

2 large eggs, lightly beaten

¾ stick (6 Tbsp.) butter, melted
and cooled

2 tsp. vanilla extract

1. Preheat oven to 325°.

2. In large mixing bowl, stir together flour, sugar, baking soda, salt, cinnamon, allspice, nutmeg, and nuts and chocolate chips if you wish.

3. In medium-sized bowl mix mashed bananas, yogurt, eggs, butter, and vanilla. Beat with electric mixer until mixture is fluffy.

4. Lightly fold wet mixture into dry ingredients. Mix with spoon just until combined and batter is thick and chunky.

5. Spoon batter into greased 9" × 5" loaf pan. Smooth surface with spatula.

6. Bake at 325° 70-75 minutes, or until loaf is golden brown and toothpick inserted in center comes out clean.

7. Cool in pan for abut 5 minutes. Then turn out and let cool on a wire rack.

NOTE

*My favorite breakfast is a slice of this banana bread,
a bowl of berry soup (page 35), and a cup of tea!*

Zucchini Nut Bread

Arlene Lehman
S. CLYDE WEAVER, INC.

Makes 3 loaves, or 30–35 servings
Prep. Time: 20 minutes   Cooking Time: 1 hour

4 eggs

1¼ cups vegetable oil

2½ cups sugar

½ tsp. baking powder

2 tsp. baking soda

1½ tsp. salt

1 Tbsp., plus 1 tsp., vanilla

3 tsp. cinnamon

¾ tsp. nutmeg

3½ cups flour

4 cups zucchini, peeled *or* unpeeled, grated

1 cup nuts, chopped

1. In a large electric mixer bowl, beat eggs until fluffy.

2. Continue beating and add oil, sugar, baking powder, baking soda, salt, vanilla, and spices.

3. Stir in flour, grated zucchini, and chopped nuts by hand.

4. Grease and flour 3 bread pans.

5. Pour batter into pans.

6. Bake at 325° for about an hour, or until a toothpick inserted in center of loaves comes out clean.

DESSERTS

Sour Cream Apple Pie

Sara Brandt
SIMPLY SWEET

Makes 2 9" pies ❧ *Prep. Time: 15 minutes* ❧ *Baking Time: 55 minutes*

Pie Filling:
2 eggs
1½ cups sugar
½ tsp. nutmeg
4 Tbsp. flour
1 pint (16 ozs.) sour cream
1 tsp. salt
2 Tbsp. vanilla
4 cups apples, peeled and sliced
2 unbaked 9" pie shells

Crumb Topping:
⅔ cup flour
⅔ cup sugar
1 stick (8 Tbsp.) butter, softened
2 Tbsp. cinnamon

1. In a large mixing bowl, mix all Pie Filling ingredients together—except apples.

2. When smooth, stir in apples.

3. Spoon into prepared pie shells.

4. Bake at 400° for 15 minutes.

5. Turn oven to 350° and bake 30 minutes.

6. Meanwhile, mix topping ingredients together in a medium-sized bowl until crumbly.

7. Sprinkle over top of pies after they've baked a total of 45 minutes.

8. Turn oven again to 400°. Bake pies 10 more minutes, or until lightly browned.

9. Let cool to room temperature before serving.

TIP

The Topping works best if the butter is not too warm and not too cold (in other words, not melted and not straight out of the fridge). When you mix the butter with the dry ingredients you want to end up with a crumbly Topping.

Double Good Blueberry Pie

Sally Lapp
AMISH CRAFTS

Makes 1 9" pie

Prep. Time: 15 minutes ❧ *Cooking Time: 10 minutes* ❧ *Chilling Time: 2–3 hours*

¾ cup sugar
3 Tbsp. cornstarch
⅛ tsp. salt
¼ cup water
4 cups fresh blueberries, *divided*
1 Tbsp. lemon juice
1 Tbsp. butter
baked 9" pie shell
whipped topping

1. Combine sugar, cornstarch, and salt in a saucepan.

2. Add water and 2 cups blueberries.

3. Cook over medium heat, stirring constantly until mixture comes to a boil and then thickens and clears.

4. Remove from heat. Stir in lemon juice and butter.

5. Cool to room temperature.

6. Place remaining 2 cups of (uncooked) berries in 9" baked pie shell.

7. Top with cooked berry mixture.

8. Chill.

9. Just before serving spoon whipped topping over berries.

Apricot Cream Pie

Sally Lapp
AMISH CRAFTS

Makes 1 9" pie

Prep. Time: 15 minutes ❦ *Cooking Time: 15 minutes* ❦ *Chilling Time: 4-5 hours*

baked 9" pie shell

1 quart fresh apricots, pitted and quartered

½–¾ cup sugar (according to your taste preference)

1½ Tbsp. cornstarch

½ cup sugar

¼ tsp. salt

1½ Tbsp. cornstarch

1¾ cups milk

¼ stick (2 Tbsp.) butter

2 egg yolks

2 Tbsp. lemon juice

whipped topping

1. Cook apricots, ½–¾ cup sugar, and 1½ Tbsp. cornstarch together in a saucepan over low heat until apricots are soft and almost dry. Stir frequently to prevent sticking.

2. Mash with a potato masher or put through a sieve.

3. Chill apricot mixture.

4. Meanwhile, mix all remaining ingredients, *except* whipped topping, together in top of a double boiler over simmering water. Cook until thickened, stirring continually.

5. Pour creamy mixture into baked pie shell. Chill until set.

6. Carefully spread chilled apricot mixture over cream after it has set.

7. Spread with whipped topping just before serving.

Mother Stover's Peach Pie

Sam Neff
S. CLYDE WEAVER, INC.

Makes 2 9" pies
Prep. Time: 20 minutes ❧ *Baking Time: 55 minutes*

3 eggs
2 9" unbaked pie shells
8 peaches
¾ cup sugar
4 Tbsp. flour
2 Tbsp. butter, melted
cinnamon

TIP

You can easily halve this recipe in order to make one pie.

1. Separate eggs.

2. Brush pie shells with some of the egg white. Bake shells (weighted with rice or dried beans) at 350° until lightly brown, about 10 minutes.

3. Meanwhile, peel and dice peaches. Set aside.

4. In a medium-sized mixing bowl blend sugar, flour, and butter. Add egg yolks.

5. In a separate mixing bowl, beat egg whites until stiff. Fold into egg-sugar mixture.

6. Put diced peaches into partially baked pie shells. Pour egg mixture over peaches. Sprinkle with cinnamon.

7. Bake at 425° for 15 minutes. Reduce oven temperature to 325° and bake another 30 minutes.

NOTE

This recipe comes from my mother-in-law who lives in Franklin County, Pennsylvania. When peaches are in season, this pie is fabulous.

Peach Raspberry Crumb Pie

Ethel Stoner

STONER'S VEGETABLES

Makes 1 9" pie

Prep. Time: 30 minutes & *Baking Time: 45-50 minutes*

3 cups ripe peaches,
peeled and sliced

1 cup sugar

1 cup red raspberries

2 Tbsp. flour

1 Tbsp. tapioca

9" unbaked pie shell

Crumb Topping:

¼ cup brown sugar

¼ cup white sugar

¾ cup flour

⅓ cup shortening

1. Mix together pie ingredients and pour into unbaked pie shell.

2. Mix Crumb Topping dry ingredients together.

3. Cut shortening into those ingredients. Crumble over fruit filling.

4. Bake at 425° for 10 minutes. Reduce heat to 375° and bake for 35 to 40 minutes, until pie filling bubbles.

During the 1930s and 1940s, Lancaster's high-society women dressed up to shop on market. I loved to watch them with their mink stoles, hats, and gloves as they bought flowers and produce from my mother. They would place their purchases in special market baskets and stroll down the aisle to make their next purchase.

— VIV HUNT, Viv's Varieties

Key Lime Pie

Sue Eshleman

Makes 1 9" pie

Prep. Time: 20 minutes ❧ Cooking Time: 15 minutes ❧ Cooling Time: 2 hours

Filling:
1 cup sugar
¼ cup flour
3 Tbsp. cornstarch
¼ tsp. salt
2 cups water
3 eggs, *separated*
1 Tbsp. butter
¼ cup fresh, *or* bottled, lime juice
grated rind of 1 lime

9" baked pie shell

Meringue Topping:
3 egg whites
¼ tsp. cream of tartar
6 Tbsp. sugar

TIP

You can use whipped topping instead of the Meringue.

NOTE

I have used this recipe for years and prefer it above the quicker versions made with sweetened condensed milk.

1. Combine first four Filling ingredients in a saucepan. Gradually stir in water.

2. Cook, stirring often until thickened. Remove from heat.

3. Place egg yolks in a medium-sized bowl. (Reserve egg whites for Meringue Topping.) Beat yolks. Gradually stir thickened mixture into yolks.

4. Return mixture to saucepan. Stir in butter, lime juice, and grated lime rind.

5. Place over low heat and cook 2 minutes, stirring continually.

6. Cool slightly.

7. Pour into baked pie shell. Cool until Filling is set, about 1½ hours.

8. Make Meringue by beating egg whites in a good-sized mixing bowl until light and frothy. Beat in cream of tartar.

9. Gradually beat in sugar, one Tbsp. at a time, until whites are stiff enough to hold a peak.

10. Spread Meringue over cooled pie filling. Spread completely to touch pastry edges to prevent Meringue from shrinking.

11. Brown Meringue-topped pie under broiler for 1 minute. (Don't forget it or it will burn.)

Lemon Sponge Pie

Wendy Hess
WENDY JO'S HOMEMADE

Makes 1 9" pie

Prep. Time: 20 minutes ❦ *Baking Time: 40–45 minutes* ❦ *Chilling Time: 3 hours*

¾ cup sugar

3 Tbsp. flour

2 eggs, *separated*

pinch of salt

1 Tbsp. butter, softened

½ cup fresh lemon juice

rind of one lemon

¾ cup milk

9" unbaked pie shell

1. In a medium-sized mixing bowl, combine sugar and flour.

2. Add slightly beaten egg yolks, salt, butter, lemon juice, and rind. Mix together.

3. Add milk. Mix well.

4. In a separate bowl, beat egg whites until stiff. Fold gently into filling.

5. Pour carefully into unbaked pie shell.

6. Bake at 375° for 20 minutes.

7. Reduce heat to 350° and bake 20–25 more minutes.

8. Check the pie periodically. If the top starts to brown, cover with a foil tent to keep it from getting too dark.

9. Chill until set. Then cut into wedges and serve.

Lemon Meringue Pie

Rose Rohrer
ROHRER'S FLOWERS

Makes 1 9" pie

Prep. Time: 20 minutes ❧ *Cooling Time: 45–60 minutes* ❧ *Baking Time: 5 minutes*

juice and rind of 3 lemons
4 eggs, *separated*
2 Tbsp. cold water
2 Tbsp. cornstarch
1 envelope unflavored gelatin
1 cup sugar, *divided*
1½ cups boiling water
1 Tbsp. butter
9" unbaked pie shell
¼ tsp. lemon extract
salt

1. Grate lemon rind into medium-sized saucepan.

2. Stir in lemon juice and egg yolks (reserve egg whites in fridge until needed below).

3. Mix cold water and cornstarch in a small bowl. When smooth, stir into lemon mixture.

4. Mix in gelatin, ¾ cup sugar, boiling water, and butter.

5. Cook until mixture bubbles, stirring constantly to keep from sticking.

6. Cool to room temperature.

7. Pour into pie shell.

8. To make meringue, beat 4 egg whites until soft peaks form.

9. Gradually beat in ¼ cup sugar, ¼ tsp. lemon extract, and a few grains of salt.

10. Spread over pie filling, making contact with the shell the whole way around the pie.

11. Bake at 425° until delicately brown, about 5 minutes.

Perfect Pumpkin Pie – Easy One-Bowl Recipe

Ruth Thomas
THOMAS PRODUCE

Makes 1 9" pie

Prep. Time: 15 minutes ❦ Baking Time: 50–60 minutes

2 cups, *or* 15-oz. can, mashed pumpkin

14-oz. can sweetened condensed milk

2 eggs

1 tsp. ground cinnamon

½ tsp. ground ginger

½ tsp. ground nutmeg

½ tsp. salt

9" unbaked pie shell

Streusel Topping, optional:

½ cup light brown sugar

½ cup unsifted flour

half a stick (4 Tbsp.) cold butter

¼ cup nuts, chopped

TIP

Canned pumpkin or fresh pumpkin purée can be used in this recipe. The fresh purée gives the pie exceptional taste.

1. Preheat oven to 425°.

2. With wire whisk, beat pumpkin, milk, eggs, spices, and salt together in a good-sized mixing bowl.

3. Pour into unbaked pie shell.

4. Bake 15 minutes.

5. Reduce oven heat to 350°. Continue baking 30 minutes.

6. If you want to add the Streusel Topping, skip to Step 7 below. If you do not want to top the pie with Streusel, bake the pie 5–10 more minutes (for a total baking time at 350° of 35–40 minutes), or until a knife inserted 1 inch from crust comes out clean.

7. Cool until set.

8. If you wish, make Streusel Topping during first 30 minutes of baking time by combining brown sugar and flour in mixing bowl.

9. Cut in butter until crumbly.

10. Stir in chopped nuts.

11. After pie has baked at 350° for 30 minutes, sprinkle Streusel on top.

12. Bake 5–10 more minutes, or until a knife inserted 1 inch from crust comes out clean.

Rhubarb Pie

Ethel Stoner
STONER'S VEGETABLES

Makes 1 9" pie
Prep. Time: 15-20 minutes ❧ *Baking Time: 55 minutes*

Crumb Topping:
¼ cup sugar
¼ cup brown sugar
¾ cup flour
⅓ cup shortening

Filling:
4 cups rhubarb, cut in ½" pieces
1¼ cups sugar
¼ cup flour
3 eggs
1 Tbsp. vanilla

9" unbaked pie shell

1. To make Crumbs, mix together sugars and flour in a mixing bowl. Cut in shortening until crumbly. Set aside.

2. In a large mixing bowl, prepare Filling by combining rhubarb with sugar and flour. Stir to coat fruit.

3. Add eggs and vanilla.

4. Spoon Filling into unbaked pie shell. Top with reserved Crumbs.

5. Bake 10 minutes at 425°. Reduce heat to 325° and bake an additional 45 minutes until pie is bubbly.

6. Cool and serve.

7. Serve with vanilla ice cream if you wish.

Coconut Cream Pie

Ruth Thomas
THOMAS PRODUCE

Makes 1 9" pie

Prep. Time: 10 minutes ❧ *Cooking Time: 12 minutes* ❧ *Baking Time: 5-7 minutes*

2 Tbsp. butter

¼ cup cornstarch

½ cup sugar

½ tsp. salt

2 cups milk

2 egg yolks, slightly beaten

1 tsp. vanilla

9" baked pie shell

¼ cup flaked coconut

Meringue:

4 egg whites

¼ tsp. cream of tarter

2½ Tbsp. sugar

1. Melt butter in medium-sized saucepan.

2. Blend cornstarch, sugar, and salt into butter.

3. Gradually add milk and heat to boiling, stirring constantly.

4. Remove from heat.

5. Place egg yolks in small bowl. Stir about ⅓ cup hot creamed mixture into yolks. When blended, pour back into creamed mixture in saucepan.

6. Return to heat and cook 2 more minutes, stirring continually.

7. Stir in vanilla.

8. Pour directly into baked pie shell.

9. To make Meringue, beat egg whites and cream of tarter together with an electric mixer until stiff peaks form.

10. Gently add sugar. Continue beating until sugar is dissolved.

11. Spread Meringue over warm pie, making sure that Meringue touches the crust completely around the pie's perimeter.

12. Sprinkle coconut over top.

13. Bake at 400° until meringue is evenly browned, about 5 minutes. Watch carefully so that the pie doesn't burn.

TIP

If you prefer, add coconut to the cooked mixture in Step 7, rather than on top (Step 12). Or add some coconut into the creamy mixture and sprinkle some over Meringue.

I've tried many different recipes for Coconut Cream Pie, but none beats this recipe.

Southern Pecan Pie

Arlene Leaman
S. CLYDE WEAVER, INC.

Makes 1 9" pie
Prep. Time: 10 minutes ❧ *Cooking Time: 10 minutes* ❧ *Baking Time: 45 minutes*

1½ cups light corn syrup
½ cup sugar
¼ cup shortening
½ tsp. salt
3 eggs, beaten
½ tsp. vanilla
1 cup pecans, chopped
9" unbaked pie shell
8 pecan halves

1. Combine corn syrup, sugar, shortening, and salt in medium-sized saucepan.

2. Bring to boil over low heat.

3. Crack eggs into medium bowl and beat.

4. Pour hot liquid slowly over beaten eggs, stirring to blend.

5. Cool slightly.

6. Add vanilla. Then stir in chopped pecans.

7. Pour mixture into pie shell.

8. Bake 10 minutes at 400°.

9. Reduce oven heat to 375°. Bake 35 more minutes.

10. Decorate top of finished pie with pecan halves, one for each slice. Be sure to do this while the pie is still hot so the pecans stick!

TIP

If pie is turning too brown before end of baking time, cover it with foil to finish.

NOTE

This pie is a favorite of our family. The last several years I've baked several over the holidays to give to neighbors instead of Christmas cookies.

Never-Fail Pastry

Ethel Stoner

STONER'S VEGETABLES

Makes 2 9" pie shells
Prep Time: 15–20 minutes

1½ cups flour
½ tsp. salt
½ cup vegetable shortening
1 egg yolk
2 Tbsp. cold water
1½ tsp. vinegar

1. Mix flour and salt in a medium-sized mixing bowl.

2. Cut in shortening until mixture resembles small peas.

3. Combine remaining ingredients in a separate bowl. Stir into shortening mixture.

4. Knead until all ingredients are thoroughly mixed and dough forms a ball.

5. Divide dough in half. Using a rolling pin, roll half of dough onto a floured board until it's large enough to fit into a 9" pie pan.

6. Fold rolled dough lightly into quarters and lift into pie pan. Unfold and fit into bottom, up the sides, and over the top edge of the pan. Cut off excess dough extending beyond the top edge. Crimp the edges.

Banana Coconut Cake

Joanne Warfel
S. CLYDE WEAVER, INC.

Makes 12 servings

Prep. Time: 30 minutes ❧ Baking Time: 25–30 minutes ❧ Cooling Time: 15 minutes

¾ cup shortening

1½ cups sugar

2 eggs

1 cup ripe bananas, mashed

1 tsp. vanilla

2 cups cake flour

1 tsp. baking soda

1 tsp. baking powder

½ tsp. salt

½ cup buttermilk

½ cup pecans, chopped, *optional*

1 cup flaked coconut

Icing:

½ cup shortening

1 stick (8 Tbsp.) butter, softened

2 cups confectioners sugar

½ tsp. vanilla

½ tsp. coconut extract

¼ cup cold evaporated milk

1. Make cake by creaming ¾ cup shortening and sugar together in large mixing bowl until fluffy.

2. Add eggs. Beat 2 minutes.

3. Add bananas and 1 tsp. vanilla. Beat another 2 minutes. Set aside.

4. Combine dry ingredients in separate bowl.

5. Add to creamed mixture alternately with buttermilk. Mix well.

6. Stir in pecans if you wish.

7. Pour into two greased, waxed-paper-lined, 9" round cake pans. Sprinkle each with coconut.

8. Bake at 375° for 25–30 minutes, or until tester inserted in centers of cakes comes out clean.

9. Loosely cover with foil for last 10 minutes of baking.

10. Cool in pans for 15 minutes.

11. Remove to wire racks, coconut-side up for final cooling.

12. While cake is cooling make Icing.

13. Cream shortening and butter together.

14. Add confectioners sugar, vanilla, coconut extract, and evaporated milk.

15. Mix on low until combined.

16. Beat on high for 5 minutes.

17. Place one cake layer upside down on serving plate.

18. Cover with frosting.

19. Place second cake on top, coconut side up.

20. Frost cake sides and 1" around perimeter of top, leaving coconut center showing.

Feather Cake

Michael L. Ervin
CENTRAL MARKET MANAGER

Makes 12 servings ❦ *Prep. Time: 20 minutes*
Baking Time: 40 minutes ❦ *Cooling Time: 1½ hours* ❦ *Broiling Time: 1–2 minutes*

1 stick butter, softened
1½ cups sugar
3 eggs, beaten
½ tsp. vanilla
2 cups cake flour
1 tsp. baking powder
1 tsp. baking soda
dash of salt
1 cup buttermilk

Frosting:
¾ stick (6 Tbsp.) butter, melted
½ cup brown sugar
¼ cup cream
½ tsp. vanilla
1 cup grated coconut

1. Make cake by creaming butter, sugar, eggs, and vanilla together in electric mixer bowl.

2. In a separate bowl sift together dry ingredients.

3. Add dry ingredients to creamed ingredients alternating with buttermilk.

4. Bake at 350° for 40 minutes in a greased 9" × 13" baking pan.

5. Combine Frosting ingredients in a good-sized mixing bowl.

6. Spread on top of cooled cake.

7. Broil until brown. Watch carefully to prevent burning!

NOTE

A friend gave me one of these cakes every year on my birthday. During her lifetime she made and gave away over one thousand of these cakes.

Alsatian Apple Cake

Henner and Heidi Steinle
THE GERMAN DELI

Makes 10-12 servings

Prep. Time: 30 minutes ❦ *Baking Time: 1 hour and 20 minutes* ❦ *Chilling Time: 2 hours*

1½ cups flour

7 Tbsp. cold butter

1 egg yolk

2 Tbsp. sugar

pinch of salt

2 Tbsp. cold water

1–1½ lbs. apples (Macintosh are great!)

2 Tbsp. lemon juice

Topping:

½ cup sugar

3 eggs

1 tsp. vanilla extract

½ cup heavy cream

1. Place flour, butter, egg yolk, sugar, salt, and water in large electric mixer bowl.

2. Knead with dough hook until all ingredients come together to form a ball.

3. Wrap in aluminum foil and refrigerate 2 hours.

4. While dough is cooling, peel and core apples. Cut into quarters.

5. Make cuts lengthwise in apple quarters, about ⅛" apart (do not cut through).

6. Brush with lemon juice.

7. Remove chilled dough from refrigerator. Place on work surface and roll out to a circle about ¼"-thick.

8. Place in a fruit cake pan. Puncture dough several times with a fork.

9. Distribute apples over top of dough, slit sides up.

10. Preheat oven to 350°. Bake 35 minutes.

11. While Cake is baking, make Topping.

12. In a mixing bowl, beat sugar and eggs until foamy.

13. Add vanilla and heavy cream. Mix well.

14. Remove Cake from oven. Pour Topping over Cake.

15. Return Cake to oven and bake an additional 40–45 minutes.

16. Allow Cake to cool in pan for 10 minutes.

17. Remove from pan and place on cooling rack.

Chocolate Raspberry Torte

Arlene Leaman
S. CLYDE WEAVER, INC.

Makes 16 servings
Prep. Time: 30 minutes ✽ Baking Time: 25-35 minutes

2 cups sugar
1 cup water
1 cup buttermilk
2 eggs
½ cup unsweetened applesauce
¼ cup canola oil
2 tsp. vanilla extract
2 cups flour
1 cup dry baking cocoa
1 tsp. baking powder
½ tsp. salt
½ tsp. baking soda

Filling:
8-oz. pkg. reduced-fat cream cheese, softened
½ cup confectioners sugar
¼ cup seedless raspberry jam

Garnish:
fresh raspberries
mint sprigs
confectioners sugar

1. In a large bowl, beat sugar, water, buttermilk, eggs, applesauce, oil, and vanilla until well blended.

2. In a separate bowl, combine flour, cocoa, baking powder, salt, and baking soda.

3. Gradually beat into sugar mixture until blended.

4. Transfer to two 9" round baking pans, coated with cooking spray.

5. Bake at 350° for 25–35 minutes, or until a toothpick inserted near the centers of cake layers comes out clean.

6. Meanwhile, in a small bowl, make Filling by beating cream cheese, confectioners sugar, and jam together until blended.

7. When cakes have cooled to room temperature, split each cake into 2 horizontal layers.

8. Place bottom layer on a serving plate.

9. Spread with one-third of Filling.

10. Repeat for next two layers.

11. Top with remaining cake layer.

12. Garnish with raspberries, mint, and confectioners sugar.

Four-Layer Pumpkin Cake

Linda Rittenhouse
TURKEY LADY

Makes 8-10 servings

Prep. Time: 30 minutes ❧ Baking Time: 28-30 minutes ❧ Cooling Time: 40 minutes

1 pkg. yellow cake mix

15-oz. can pumpkin, *divided*

½ cup milk

⅓ cup oil

4 eggs

1½ tsp. pumpkin pie spice, *divided*

8-oz. pkg. cream cheese, softened

1 cup confectioners sugar

8-oz. container whipped topping, thawed

¼ cup caramel ice cream topping

¼ cup chopped pecans

1. Heat oven to 350°.

2. Grease and flour two 9" round baking pans.

3. Beat cake mix, 1 cup pumpkin, milk, oil, eggs, and 1 tsp. spice in large bowl with mixer until well blended.

4. Pour batter into prepared pans.

5. Bake 28–30 minutes, or until toothpick inserted in centers comes out clean.

6. Cool in pans for 10 minutes.

7. Remove from pans to wire racks. Cool completely.

8. Meanwhile, beat cream cheese in small bowl with mixer until creamy.

9. Add confectioners sugar, remaining pumpkin, and reserved spice. Mix well.

10. Gently fold in whipped topping.

11. Cut each cake layer in half horizontally with a serrated knife.

12. Spread ⅓ of cream cheese filling on top of first layer. Stack second cake layer on top of filling.

13. Repeat steps 11 and 12 with remaining two layers. *Leave top of upper layer unfrosted.*

14. Drizzle with caramel topping.

15. Sprinkle with nuts.

16. Refrigerate until ready to serve.

Sour Cream Rhubarb Cake

Ethel Stoner
STONER'S VEGETABLES

Makes 16-20 servings
Prep. Time: 15-20 minutes ✣ *Baking Time: 40 minutes*

half a stick (4 Tbsp.) butter, softened

1½ cups brown sugar, firmly packed

1 egg

1 Tbsp. vanilla

2⅓ cups flour

1 tsp. baking soda

1 tsp. salt

1 cup sour cream

4 cups red rhubarb, cut in ½" pieces

½ cup sugar

½ tsp. nutmeg

1. In a large electric mixing bowl, cream butter and brown sugar until fluffy.

2. Beat in egg and vanilla.

3. In a separate bowl, sift flour with baking soda and salt. Stir into sugar/egg mixture until well blended. (Batter will be stiff!)

4. Fold in sour cream and rhubarb.

5. Spoon into greased 9" × 13" baking pan.

6. In a small bowl, mix sugar and nutmeg together. Sprinkle over batter.

7. Bake 40 minutes at 350°, or until tester inserted in center of cake comes out clean.

Shoppers leaving the Market with full baskets often found their burdens too great to bear. In years gone by, enterprising boys and a few girls waited with their express wagons (or sometimes sleds in winter) around the Market to offer their assistance. Few of these youngsters were over 12 years old.

Strawberry Swirl Cake

Joyce Denlinger
S. CLYDE WEAVER, INC.

Makes 16 servings

Prep. Time: 30–50 minutes ❧ *Baking Time: 28–30 minutes* ❧ *Cooling Time: 45–60 minutes*

1 box white cake mix (2-layer size)

1 pkg. strawberry gelatin (4-servings size)

Topping:

1 cup sour cream

1 cup confectioners sugar

12-oz. container whipped topping, thawed

2½ cups strawberries, sliced

1. Preheat oven to 350°.

2. Grease 2 round cake pans, 8 or 9 inches in diameter

3. Prepare cake batter as directed on package.

4. Pour *half* the batter into a large mixing bowl.

5. Add dry gelatin mix. Stir until well blended.

6. Spoon half the white batter and half the pink batter side-by-side into each baking pan.

7. Gently pull a table knife through the two batters to create a "streaked" pink-white batter.

8. Bake 30 minutes. Then allow to cool to room temperature.

9. While cake is baking, mix sour cream and confectioners sugar in a medium-sized mixing bowl until well blended.

10. Fold in whipped topping.

11. Place one cooled cake layer on a serving plate.

12. Spread 1 cup Topping on top of cake layer.

13. Place 1 cup sliced strawberries on Topping.

14. Place second cake layer on top of first.

15. Spread remaining topping on sides and top of cake.

16. Place remaining strawberries on top of cake just before serving.

17. Refrigerate until ready to serve.

TESTER TIP

I made this cake for a 16th birthday party. I used tiny fresh berries to ring the outer edge of the top of the cake and to make a "16" in the center of the top!

Zucchini Cake

Sally Lapp
AMISH CRAFTS

Makes 16-20 servings

Prep. Time: 20-25 minutes ❧ *Baking Time: 45-50 minutes* ❧ *Cooling Time: 1-1½ hours*

2 cups flour
2 cups sugar
1 Tbsp. cinnamon
2 tsp. baking soda
1 tsp. baking powder
1 tsp. salt
1 cup oil
2 tsp. vanilla
3 eggs
2 cups unpeeled, grated zucchini
1 cup raisins
1½ cups chopped nuts, *divided*

Glaze:
2 Tbsp. melted butter
2 Tbsp. milk
¾ cup confectioners sugar, *or* enough to thicken glaze to spreadable consistency

1. In large electric mixing bowl combine flour, sugar, cinnamon, baking soda, baking powder, salt, oil, vanilla, and eggs.

2. Beat at medium speed until well mixed.

3. Stir in zucchini, raisins, and 1 cup nuts.

4. Pour into greased 9" × 13" baking pan.

5. Sprinkle with remaining half cup of nuts.

6. Bake in preheated oven at 350° for 45–50 minutes, or until tester inserted in center of cake comes out clean.

7. While cake is baking, stir glaze ingredients together in medium-sized bowl.

8. When baked cake has reached room temperature, pour glaze over top.

Family Favorite Cheesecake

Arlene Leaman
S. CLYDE WEAVER, INC.

Makes 12 servings ❧ *Prep. Time: 30 minutes*
Baking Time: 65 minutes ❧ *Chilling Time: 4¼ hours plus overnight, or 12¼ hours total*

Crust:

2½ cups graham cracker crumbs (about 40 squares)

⅓ cup sugar

½ tsp. cinnamon

1 stick (8 Tbsp.) butter, melted

Filling:

3 8-oz. pkgs. cream cheese, softened

1½ cups sugar

1 tsp. vanilla extract

4 eggs, separated

Topping:

½ cup sour cream

2 Tbsp. sugar

½ tsp. vanilla extract

½ cup whipping cream

1. In medium-sized bowl combine cracker crumbs, ⅓ cup sugar, and cinnamon.

2. Stir in butter.

3. Press onto bottom and 2 inches up the side of greased 9" springform pan.

4. Bake at 350° for 5 minutes.

5. Cool on a wire rack.

6. Reduce heat to 325°.

7. In a good-sized electric mixer bowl, beat cream cheese, 1½ cups sugar, and 1 tsp. vanilla until smooth.

8. Add egg yolks. Beat on low just until combined.

9. In a small mixing bowl beat egg whites until soft peaks form. Fold into cream cheese mixture.

10. Spoon over crust, being careful not to disturb crumbs.

11. Bake 1 hour, or until center is set.

12. Cool on a wire rack 10 minutes.

13. Carefully pass a knife around edge of pan to loosen.

14. Cool an additional hour.

15. Refrigerate until completely cooled.

16. Meanwhile, combine sour cream, 2 Tbsp. sugar, and ½ tsp. vanilla. Fold in whipping cream.

17. Spread over cheesecake.

18. Refrigerate overnight.

19. Remove sides of pan when ready to serve.

TIP

I like to serve this with a spoonful of fresh strawberries or cherry pie filling over each individual serving.

Potomac Pound Cake

Karen Paul
S. CLYDE WEAVER, INC.

Makes 12 servings
Prep. Time: 15-20 minutes ❧ Baking Time: 1-1¼ hours

2 sticks (16 Tbsp.) butter, softened

1½–3 cups sugar, according to your taste preference

6 large eggs

½ tsp. vanilla

¼ tsp. orange extract

¼ tsp. fresh lemon juice, *or* extract

3 cups flour

½ tsp. baking soda

1 cup sour cream, *or* ricotta cheese

TIP

This is great topped with a fruit sauce or served with ice cream, or with slices toasted and spread with butter.

1. Preheat oven to 325°.

2. In an electric mixer bowl, cream butter and sugar together until fluffy.

3. Beat in eggs, one at a time, mixing well after each addition.

4. Add vanilla, orange extract, and lemon juice or extract.

5. In separate bowl sift flour and baking soda together.

6. Alternately add flour mixture and sour cream to creamed mixture.

7. Beat at medium speed for 10 minutes.

8. Pour into greased loaf pan.

9. Bake 1-1¼ hours, or until toothpick inserted in center comes out clean.

Apple Cheesecake with Streusel

Henner and Heidi Steinle

THE GERMAN DELI

Makes 10 servings ❦ *Prep. Time: 50 minutes*
Baking Time: 50 minutes ❦ *Chilling Time: 1 hour* ❦ *Resting Time: 1¼ hours*

Dough:

⅓ cup sugar

1 stick plus 2 Tbsp. (10 Tbsp.) butter, softened

1¼ cups flour

1 tsp. baking powder

1 egg

zest of half a lemon

pinch of salt

Filling:

1 cup ricotta cheese

½ cup sour cream

1 egg

1 egg yolk

1 tsp. vanilla

2 Tbsp. sugar

Topping:

½ cup ground hazelnuts

¼ cup golden raisins

3 large apples, peeled, cored, and sectioned

Streusel:

2 cups flour

½ cup sugar

1½ tsp. cinnamon

1½ sticks (12 Tbsp.) butter, melted

1. Before mixing Dough, place ricotta in large sieve over bowl. Allow to drain while preparing and chilling Dough.

2. In a large mixing bowl, prepare Dough by mixing sugar and butter together with a pastry blender.

3. When small pea-sized crumbs form, add rest of Dough ingredients and knead lightly with hands.

4. Cover and place in refrigerator 1 hour.

5. Meanwhile, cover bottom of 11" or 12" spring-form pan with greased parchment paper.

6. Roll out chilled Dough to size of springform-pan bottom. Fold lightly into quarters and place in greased pan. Fit Dough into pan bottom.

7. To make Filling, combine drained ricotta with sour cream in a good-sized mixing bowl.

8. Stir egg and egg yolk into Filling. Stir in vanilla and sugar. Set aside.

9. Spread hazelnuts evenly over dough.

10. Cover nuts with dollops of Filling. Spread evenly, being careful not to disturb nuts.

11. Distribute raisins evenly over Filling.

recipe continues on the next page of text

12. Peel, core, and slice apples. Distribute apple slices evenly over top of raisins.

13. Bake 30 minutes at 350°.

14. While cake is baking, prepare Streusel by mixing flour, sugar, and cinnamon together in a large bowl.

15. Add melted butter. Toss with 2 forks until just mixed.

16. Remove cake from oven. Sprinkle Streusel over top of cake.

17. Return to oven and bake 20 more minutes.

18. Remove cake from oven and let rest 15 minutes on cooling rack.

19. Use a sharp knife to remove edge of pan from cake. Allow to cool thoroughly before serving.

Date and Nut Cake

Edith Groff
GROFF'S HOMEGROWN VEGETABLES

Makes about 10 servings
Prep. Time: 20 minutes   Baking Time: 35–45 minutes

1 cup sugar
1 Tbsp. butter, softened
1 egg
1 cup chopped dates
1 scant tsp. baking soda
1 cup boiling water
1½ cups flour
1 tsp. vanilla
1 cup chopped English walnuts

1. Mix sugar, butter, and egg together in a good-sized mixing bowl until thoroughly combined.

2. In a separate bowl, sprinkle baking soda over chopped dates. Add boiling water and mix.

3. When well combined, stir into sugar mixture.

4. Stir in flour, vanilla and nuts and mix together thoroughly.

5. Pour into lightly greased 9" square baking pan.

6. Bake at 350° for 35–45 minutes, or until toothpick inserted in center of cake comes out clean.

Moravian Sugar Cake

Rose Rohrer
ROHRER'S FLOWERS

Makes 30 servings
Prep. Time: 35 minutes ❧ Baking Time: 20 minutes ❧ Rising Time: 2¼ hours

2 cups milk
⅔ cup shortening
1 pkg. yeast
½ cup warm water
⅔ cup sugar, *divided*
2 tsp. salt
6½ cups flour

Brown Sugar Topping:
1 cup brown sugar
¾ stick (6 Tbsp.) butter, melted
¼ cup flour

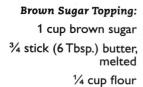

1. In a small saucepan heat milk and shortening over low heat until shortening melts. Set aside.

2. In a small bowl, combine water and yeast and 1 tsp. sugar until bubbly.

3. In a large bowl, combine yeast and milk mixture with salt and remaining sugar.

4. Gradually add flour to make a soft dough.

5. Knead about 5 minutes, adding flour as necessary.

6. Cover with a tea towel. Let rise in a warm place until about double in size, about 1½ hours.

7. Divide dough into 2 parts. Spread each part onto a greased baking sheet. Flatten with the heel of your hand to about ½" high.

8. Cover with a tea towel. Let rise on baking sheets in a warm place for 45 minutes.

9. Make holes with your finger spaced about 2 inches apart throughout the dough.

10. Make Topping by combining brown sugar, butter, and flour with a fork in a small bowl.

11. Fill holes with brown sugar crumbs. Sprinkle remainder over top.

12. Bake at 350° for 20 minutes. Watch closely after 15 minutes to make sure it doesn't get too brown.

13. When the cake is warm, but no longer hot, cut into 3" squares and serve.

Bountiful Bread Pudding

Sue Glouner
TURKEY LADY

Makes 20 servings
Prep. Time: 20-25 minutes ✣ *Baking Time: 1 hour and 15 minutes*

Bread Pudding:

10-oz. loaf stale French bread, broken, *or* 8 cups of any white *or* whole wheat bread

4 cups milk, *or* 2 cups milk and 2 cups cream

2 cups sugar

1 stick (8 Tbsp. butter), melted

3 eggs

2 Tbsp. vanilla

1 cup raisins

1 cup shredded coconut

1 cup chopped pecans

1 tsp. cinnamon

1 tsp. nutmeg

Sauce:

1 stick (8 Tbsp.) butter

1½ cups confectioners sugar

1 egg, separated

½ cup bourbon, *optional*

1. In a very large mixing bowl, combine all Pudding ingredients, stirring well until mixture is quite moist throughout but not soupy.

2. Spoon into buttered 9" × 13" baking dish.

3. Place on middle rack of non-preheated oven.

4. Bake at 350° for 1 hour and 15 minutes, or until top is golden brown.

5. While Pudding is baking, prepare Sauce by melting butter and mixing in sugar over medium heat. Stir constantly until well blended.

6. Remove from heat.

7. Pour 2–4 Tbsp. blended butter-sugar mixture into egg yolk in a medium bowl (save white for another use). Stir together well. Add rest of butter-sugar mixture, stirring until well blended.

8. If you wish, pour in bourbon to taste, stirring constantly.

9. Sauce will thicken as it cools.

10. Serve Pudding warm, or at room temperature, along with cooled Sauce.

Panettone Bread Pudding with Amaretto Sauce

Sally Delgiorno
DELGIORNO'S ITALIAN SPECIALTIES

Makes 10 servings

Prep. Time: 20 minutes ❧ Standing Time: 30 minutes ❧ Baking Time: 45 minutes

Bread Pudding:

1-lb. loaf panettone bread,
crusts removed
8 large eggs
1½ cups whipping cream
2½ cups milk
1¼ cups sugar

Amaretto Sauce:

½ cup whipping cream
½ cup milk
3 Tbsp. sugar
¼ cup amaretto liqueur
2 tsp. cornstarch

1. Cut bread into 1" cubes. Place in a greased 9" × 13" baking pan.

2. In a large bowl make pudding mixture by whisking together eggs, cream, milk, and sugar until sugar is dissolved.

3. Pour mixture over bread cubes.

4. Press bread cubes gently to submerge in liquid.

5. Let stand 30 minutes, pushing down occasionally on bread cubes to keep submerged.

6. Preheat oven to 350°.

7. Bake until Pudding puffs and is set in the center, about 45 minutes.

8. While Pudding is baking, make Amaretto Sauce.

9. Combine cream, milk, and sugar in a small, heavy saucepan.

10. Bring to a boil over medium heat, stirring constantly.

11. In a small bowl, combine amaretto and cornstarch.

12. Blend with whisk, and then whisk into cream mixture.

13. Simmer over medium-low heat until sauce thickens, about 2 minutes, stirring constantly.

14. Set aside and keep warm.

15. When Bread Pudding is slightly cooled, spoon into serving bowls.

16. Drizzle with warm Amaretto Sauce and serve.

Apple Crisp

Janelle Glick
LANCASTER GENERAL WELLNESS PARTNERSHIP

Makes 6 servings

Prep. Time: 20 minutes 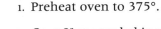 *Cooking Time: 50 minutes* *Cooling Time: 20 minutes or more*

4 Granny Smith apples

½ cup raisins

3 Tbsp. apple juice

¼ cup whole wheat flour

¼ cup dry rolled oats

¼ cup brown sugar

¾ tsp. ground cinnamon

¾ tsp. ground nutmeg

¾ Tbsp. cold butter, cut into small pieces

NOTE

This is a dessert that's a treat for your health as well as your taste buds.

1. Preheat oven to 375°.

2. Coat 8" square baking pan with cooking spray (preferably canola oil spray).

3. Core apples and cut into thin slices or bite-size pieces.

4. Combine apples, raisins, and apple juice in bowl. Toss well and set aside.

5. In another bowl, combine flour, dry rolled oats, brown sugar, cinnamon, and nutmeg.

6. With pastry blender or knife and fork, cut butter into oats mix until mixture forms coarse crumbs.

7. Transfer apple mixture to baking pan. Sprinkle crumbs evenly over fruit and lightly coat with cooking spray.

8. Cover with foil and bake 30 minutes.

9. Uncover and bake 20 minutes more, or until apples are tender.

10. Remove from oven and let stand on wire rack at least 20 minutes.

11. Cut into squares and serve warm or at room temperature.

Apple Cinnamon Tarts

Ruthie Houser
MECK'S PRODUCE

Makes 6-8 servings
Prep. Time: 30 minutes ❦ *Cooking Time: 25-30 minutes*

1 cup sugar
1 cup water
4 tsp. cornstarch
4 tsp. cold water
6–8 apples, peeled and sliced
1½ cups flour
2 tsp. baking powder
½ tsp. salt
¼ cup shortening
¾ cup milk
2 Tbsp. butter, melted
2 Tbsp. sugar
½ tsp. cinnamon

1. In a small saucepan, boil a cup of sugar in a cup of water to make syrup. Stir frequently to prevent sticking and scorching.

2. In a small bowl, mix cornstarch with 4 tsp. cold water. When smooth, stir into hot syrup. Continue cooking and stirring over low heat until syrup thickens slightly.

3. Place apple slices in an 8" × 8" greased baking pan.

4. Pour syrup over apples.

5. In a good-sized mixing bowl, sift together flour, baking powder, and salt.

6. Cut in shortening.

7. Stir in milk to make a soft dough.

8. Drop by spoonfuls over top of apples.

9. Make a dent in the top of each dollop.

10. Melt butter. Mix with 2 Tbsp. sugar and cinnamon.

11. Spoon topping into each dent.

12. Bake for 25–30 minutes at 400°.

13. Serve warm with milk.

TIP

I use Gala apples and they stay firm but aren't crunchy. Excellent!

Rhubarb Crunch

Ethel Stoner
STONER'S VEGETABLES

Makes 6-8 servings
Prep. Time: 15 minutes ❧ *Baking Time: 40 minutes*

Fruit Mixture:

4 cups rhubarb, cut in 1" pieces

¾ cup sugar, or less if you prefer a more tart dessert

2 Tbsp. flour

1 tsp. cinnamon

Topping:

¾ cup dry rolled oats

¾ cup brown sugar

3 Tbsp. shortening

1. Prepare Fruit by combining rhubarb, sugar, flour, and cinnamon in a mixing bowl.

2. Spoon into greased 8" square baking dish.

3. In the same mixing bowl, combine dry oats and brown sugar. Cut in shortening.

4. Sprinkle over rhubarb.

5. Bake 40 minutes at 375°.

6. Serve warm with milk or vanilla ice cream.

When I was a small child, my mother took me along to her market stand. One day she went to Watt & Shand, our former department store, to buy yarn and needles. She came back to market and proceeded to teach me how to knit. I guess she thought that would keep me busy, plus keep me out of trouble.

— FRANCES KIEFER, Kiefer's Meats

Mango Sticky Rice

NARAI THAI CUISINE

Makes 3–4 servings ❧ *Prep. Time: 2 hours*
Soaking Time: 20–60 minutes ❧ *Cooking Time: 30 minutes* ❧ *Standing/Chilling Time: 1 hour*

1 cup dry Thai sweet rice
1¾ cups water
1 can coconut milk, *divided*
½ cup sugar, *divided*
¼ tsp. salt, *divided*
2 fresh mangoes
¼ tsp. sesame seed

1. Soak sweet rice in a good-sized saucepan in water for 20–60 minutes before cooking.

2. Do not drain water off rice. Stir ½ can coconut milk, ¼ cup sugar, and dash of salt into water-rice mixture. Stir up from the bottom, making sure no rice is sticking to bottom of pan.

3. Cover and bring to a boil. Reduce heat to medium-low and allow to simmer for about 20 minutes, or until rice has absorbed all the liquid. Set aside.

4. Peel mangoes and cut into small pieces. Refrigerate until ready to use.

5. Make coconut sauce by bringing remaining ½ can coconut milk, remaining ¼ cup sugar, and remaining salt just to a boil in a small saucepan. Remove from heat immediately.

6. Allow sauce to reach room temperature. Then chill in refrigerator for at least 30 minutes.

7. To serve, put 1 scoop steamed sweet rice on each serving plate. Top with mango, and then pour a bit of coconut sauce over top. Sprinkle with sesame seeds.

Espresso Mousse

Regine Ibold
THE SPICE STAND

Makes 10–12 servings ❧ *Prep. Time: 15–20 minutes*
Cooking Time: 20 minutes ❧ *Cooling Time: 1 hour* ❧ *Chilling Time: 9 hours, or overnight*

Mousse Ingredients:

6 egg yolks

½ cup sugar

1½ cups prepared espresso coffee

2 envelopes unflavored gelatin

½ cup cold water

1½ cups heavy cream

Sauce Ingredients:

⅔ cup sugar

1 cup prepared espresso coffee, heated

1 Tbsp. arrowroot

1 Tbsp. cold water

1 Tbsp. cognac

shaved chocolate

NOTE

Light as a cloud, this lovely rich dessert uses French roast espresso beans in a new way!

1. Beat egg yolks with ½ cup sugar. Stir in coffee.

2. Pour into saucepan. Cook over low heat, stirring constantly, until mixture forms a thin custard.

3. Remove from heat.

4. In a small bowl, soften gelatin in ½ cup cold water. Blend thoroughly into custard. Let cool.

5. Whip cream in a separate bowl. When custard reaches room temperature, fold in whipped cream.

6. Rinse a 2-quart mold with cold water. Spoon Mousse into it.

7. Cover filled mold with plastic wrap. Chill 9 hours, or overnight.

8. Prepare Sauce by dissolving ⅔ cup sugar in hot coffee in saucepan.

9. In small bowl, mix arrowroot with 1 Tbsp. cold water to form thin paste.

10. Stir into sweetened espresso. Cook, stirring constantly, until Sauce becomes clear and thickened.

11. Stir in cognac.

12. Chill Sauce, covered with plastic wrap.

13. When ready to serve, unmold Mousse. Top with Sauce and shaved chocolate, if you wish.

Blueberry Cheesecake Dessert

Faye Hess
WILLOW VALLEY BAKERY

Makes about 10-12 servings ❧ *Prep. Time: 20-30 minutes*
Cooking Time: 10-12 minutes ❧ *Cooling Time: 1 hour* ❧ *Chilling Time: 3-4 hours*

2 cups graham cracker crumbs
1½ cups sugar, *divided*
half stick (4 Tbsp.) butter, softened
8-oz. pkg. cream cheese, softened
¼ cup milk
4 cups whipped topping
2 cups confectioners sugar
4 Tbsp. cornstarch
2 cups water
1 quart blueberries

1. In a good-sized mixing bowl, mix graham cracker crumbs, ½ cup sugar, and butter together. Pat into bottom of greased 9" × 13" baking dish.

2. In an electric mixer bowl, beat together cream cheese and milk until smooth. Fold in whipped topping and confectioners sugar.

3. Spoon over top of crumbs.

4. In a good-sized saucepan, mix together 1 cup sugar and cornstarch. Stir in water until smooth. Stir in berries.

5. Cook in saucepan until thickened, stirring often.

6. Cool blueberry mixture to room temperature. Spoon over top of dessert.

7. Refrigerate until thoroughly chilled.

8. Cut into bars and serve.

Banana Cream Dessert

Liz Lapp
DUTCH COUNTRY DELI

Makes 15 servings

Prep. Time: 20 minutes ❧ *Baking Time: 10 minutes* ❧ *Cooling Time: 30–60 minutes*

Crust:

1 cup flour

1 stick (8 Tbsp.) butter, melted

Filling:

8-oz. pkg. cream cheese, softened

1 cup confectioners sugar

12-oz. container whipped topping, thawed, *divided*

6 just-ripe bananas, sliced, *divided*

4-oz. box vanilla pudding (prepared according to package directions)

1. In a mixing bowl, mix flour and melted butter for crust. Spread in bottom of 9" × 13" baking pan.

2. Bake at 350° for 10 minutes. Cool to room temperature.

3. In an electric mixer bowl, beat cream cheese until soft. Fold in confectioners sugar and 1 cup whipped topping.

4. Spread on cooled crust.

5. Place 4 sliced bananas evenly across top of cream cheese mixture.

6. Spoon prepared vanilla pudding over top of bananas.

7. Spread remaining whipped topping over pudding.

8. Garnish with 2 sliced bananas.

No-Bake Chocolate Chip Cookie Pie

Susan Stoeckl
SUSAN'S SECRET GARDEN

Makes 8 servings
Prep. Time: 20 minutes ❦ Chilling Time: 8 hours

15 oz. bag chocolate chip cookies, *divided*

1 cup milk

9-oz. pre-made graham cracker crust pie shell

8-oz. container frozen whipped topping, thawed, *divided*

1. Dip 8 cookies in milk and place in a single layer in pie shell.

2. Cover with ⅓ of whipped topping.

3. Dip 8 more cookies in milk and make a second layer in pie shell.

4. Cover with half the remaining whipped topping.

5. Dip 8 more cookies in milk and make a third layer in pie shell.

6. Cover with balance of whipped topping.

7. Crumble 2 chocolate chip cookies. Sprinkle over top of pie.

8. Cover and chill for 8 hours.

VARIATION

Use 1 lb. of your favorite homemade chocolate chip cookies instead of store-bought ones.

NOTE

Children love to help make this pie. Even though it has only four ingredients, you'll be surprised at how tasty it is—and easy!

Oreo Crumb Ice Cream Dessert

Cindy High
SPRING GLEN

Makes 15 servings
Prep. Time: 25–30 minutes ❧ *Freezing Time: 2–3 hours*

**16-oz. pkg. Oreo, *or other
chocolate sandwich cookies,
divided***

**½ gallon vanilla ice cream,
softened**

jar of caramel topping

8-oz. container whipped topping

chocolate sprinkles

1. Separate cookies and rub off cream. Crush cookies into a mixture of fine and chunky crumbs.

2. Spread half the crumbs in bottom of 9"×13" baking dish.

3. Slightly soften ice cream. Spoon, or cut into chunks, and lay over crumbs. Allow to melt further until spreadable. Gently spread over crumbs, being careful not to disturb crumbs.

4. Drizzle caramel topping over ice cream.

5. Spoon remaining cookie crumbs evenly over top.

6. Spread whipped topping over top.

7. Add chocolate sprinkles.

8. Freeze until ready to serve, at least 2–3 hours.

Rhubarb Sauce

Ethel Stoner
STONER'S VEGETABLES

Makes 6–8 servings

Prep. Time: 10 minutes ❧ Cooking Time: 20–30 minutes ❧ Cooling Time: 2 hours

6–8 cups rhubarb, cut in 1" pieces
1 cup water
1½ cups sugar
2 Tbsp. instant tapioca

VARIATION

Substitute .3-oz. pkg. strawberry gelatin in place of tapioca. This makes the sauce a beautiful red.

1. Wash rhubarb and cut into 1" pieces.

2. Put rhubarb in saucepan with water and sugar. Bring to boil and simmer until tender, 20–30 minutes. Stir occasionally.

3. Remove from heat. Immediately add tapioca, stirring until well mixed.

4. Cool and serve.

 Fifty years ago when I was a little girl, my mother and I would board a bus in Lititz and travel to Lancaster. We went to the Plain Clothing Department of Hager's Department Store to deliver ladies bonnets that Mother had sewn at home. After Mother received her pay and the next week's orders, we crossed the street to Central Market. Mother would buy horseradish to be eaten with fresh sausage and potatoes, one of my dad's favorite meals. Today I still enjoy that wonderful aroma of freshly ground horseradish at Central Market.

— J. LORRAINE LAPP, Minnich's Farm Bakery

Rhubarb Tapioca

Ruth Thomas
THOMAS PRODUCE

Makes 6-8 servings ❧ *Prep. Time: 10 minutes*
Resting Time: 15-20 minutes ❧ *Cooking Time: 25 minutes* ❧ *Cooling/Chilling Time: 2 hours*

3 cups rhubarb, diced

1½ cups water

3 Tbsp. quick-cooking tapioca

1 cup sugar

¼ tsp. salt

3 drops red food coloring,
optional

1. Mix rhubarb, water, and tapioca in a medium-sized saucepan.

2. Let rest for 15–20 minutes.

3. Cook, stirring constantly until tapioca dissolves and is clear.

4. Boil for 15 minutes, stirring constantly.

5. Add sugar, salt, and coloring if you wish.

6. Stir over heat for several minutes.

7. Cool. When pudding reaches room temperature, refrigerate until completely chilled.

TIP

I like to stir 1 cup sliced fresh strawberries into the pudding just before serving. Or I serve the pudding in parfait glasses. I put sliced strawberries in the bottom of each glass, and then top them with sauce, and finish each with a spoon of whipped cream. When I have fresh mint, I add a couple of leaves to each glass as a garnish on the very top.

Spanish Cream

Anna Marie Groff
ANNA MARIE GROFF'S FLOWERS

Makes 10 servings

Prep. Time: 30 minutes ❦ *Cooking Time: 15 minutes* ❦ *Cooling Time: overnight, or 8 hours*

2 envelopes unflavored gelatin

3 cups cold milk

3 eggs, *separated*

½ cup sugar

¼ tsp. salt

1–2 tsp. vanilla

pineapple slices *or* other fruit of your choice

1. In a medium-sized saucepan, dissolve gelatin in cold milk over low heat.

2. Separate eggs. Beat yolks in a small bowl.

3. In a separate bowl, beat whites until stiff peaks form. Refrigerate until needed.

4. Stir sugar, beaten egg yolks, salt, and vanilla into gelatin-milk mixture in saucepan.

5. Bring to a boil over medium heat, stirring constantly.

6. When mixture reaches a boil, remove from heat. Fold in stiffly beaten egg whites.

7. Pour into 4- or 5-cup mold. When mixture reaches room temperature, cover and refrigerate overnight, or for at least 8 hours.

8. When ready to serve, loosen from mold by passing a knife around edge of mold.

9. Invert mold onto serving plate.

10. Garnish with pineapple slices or other fruit of your choice.

Oatmeal Chocolate Chip Cookies

Margie Shaffer
S. CLYDE WEAVER, INC.

Makes about 8 dozen cookies
Prep. Time: 10–12 minutes ❧ *Baking Time: 7–8 minutes per baking sheet*

1 cup shortening

1 stick (8 Tbsp.) butter, *or* margarine

1½ cups sugar

1½ cups brown sugar

2 tsp. vanilla

4 beaten eggs

2 tsp. baking soda

2 tsp. salt

4 cups flour

3 cups dry quick oats

2 cups chocolate chips

1. Preheat oven to 375°.

2. In large electric mixing bowl, cream together shortening, butter, and sugars. Beat till fluffy.

3. Add vanilla, eggs, baking soda, salt, and flour. Mix well.

4. Stir in oats by hand and mix well.

5. Stir in chocolate chips by hand. Mix until well distributed throughout batter.

6. Drop by spoonfuls onto greased baking sheets.

7. Bake for 7–8 minutes. (Be careful not to over-bake.)

8. Let cool 3–4 minutes on baking sheets. Then remove cookies to wire racks to cool completely.

Cranberry-Orange Pinwheels

Rose Meck
MECK'S PRODUCE

Makes 3 dozen cookies

Prep. Time: 30 minutes ❦ *Chilling Time: 5–25 hours* ❦ *Baking Time: 8–10 minutes*

2 sticks (16 Tbsp.) butter, softened

1½ cups sugar

½ tsp. baking powder

½ tsp. salt

2 eggs

2 tsp. finely shredded orange peel

3 cups flour

confectioners sugar

Filling:

1 cup cranberries

1 cup pecans

¼ cup brown sugar, packed

1. In large electric mixer bowl, beat butter on medium to high speed for 30 seconds.

2. Add sugar, baking powder, and salt. Beat until thoroughly combined.

3. Beat in eggs and orange peel until well mixed.

4. Beat in as much flour as possible with mixer.

5. Stir in remaining flour by hand.

6. Divide dough in half.

7. Cover and chill for an hour, or until easy to handle.

8. Make Filling by chopping cranberries, pecans, and brown sugar in blender or food processor. Set aside.

9. Roll half the dough into a 10" square between sheets of waxed paper.

10. Remove waxed paper.

11. Spread half the Filling to within ½" of edges of cookie dough square. Press Filling down lightly onto dough.

12. Roll up dough.

13. Moisten edges and pinch to seal shut.

14. Dust with confectioners sugar and wrap in plastic wrap or waxed paper.

15. Make a second roll by repeating steps 9 through 14.

16. Chill 4–24 hours, or until rolls are easily cut in cross-sections.

17. Cut rolls into ¼"-thick slices.

18. Place 2 inches apart on lightly greased baking sheets.

19. Bake at 350° for 8–10 minutes, or until edges and bottoms of cookies are lightly browned.

20. Allow to cool one minute on baking sheet. Then remove to wire racks to cool fully.

Soft Ginger Cookies

Anna Marie Groff
ANNA MARIE GROFF'S FLOWERS

Makes 6 dozen

Prep. Time: 25 minutes ❧ Chilling Time: 4–5 hours ❧ Baking Time: 12–14 minutes per sheet

1 cup shortening
2 cups brown sugar
6 cups flour
2 large eggs, beaten
3 tsp. baking soda
1 tsp. salt
2 cups buttermilk
2 tsp. ground ginger
1 tsp. vanilla
1 tsp. ground cinnamon
¼–½ tsp. ground cloves
¼–½ tsp. ground nutmeg
1 cup light blackstrap molasses
1 egg

1. In a large electric mixing bowl, combine all ingredients thoroughly, except the final egg.

2. Cover and chill in refrigerator for several hours.

3. Drop by spoonfuls onto lightly greased cookie sheet, about 2 inches apart.

4. Beat single egg in a small bowl.

5. Brush each unbaked cookie with egg just before baking.

6. Bake at 350° for 12–14 minutes per sheet. Allow to cool 2 minutes on baking sheet. Remove to wire rack and cool completely before storing.

NOTE

The brushed egg gives each cookie a shiny glow when it's finished baking.

Pumpkin Cookies

Ethel Stoner
STONER'S VEGETABLES

Makes 3-4 dozen

Prep. Time: 15-25 minutes ❧ Cooking Time: 10-15 minutes per baking sheet

Cookies:

2 cups sugar

⅔ cup oil

2 cups cooked and mashed pumpkin

4 cups flour

2 tsp. baking soda

2 tsp. baking powder

2 tsp. cinnamon

1 tsp. ground cloves

1 tsp. vanilla

1 cup raisins, *or* 1 cup chocolate chips

½ cup broken nuts, *optional*

Caramel Frosting:

3 Tbsp. butter

4 tsp. milk

½ cup brown sugar

¾ tsp. vanilla

1-1¼ cups confectioners sugar

1. Preheat oven to 375°.

2. Prepare Cookies by mixing sugar, oil, and pumpkin in a big bowl.

3. In a separate bowl, combine flour, baking soda, baking powder, cinnamon, and cloves.

4. Slowly add dry ingredients and vanilla to pumpkin mixture, mixing thoroughly while doing so.

5. Fold in raisins or chocolate chips and nuts, if you wish.

6. Drop on greased cookie sheet by tablespoonfuls, about 1" apart from each other.

7. Bake 10-15 minutes per baking sheet.

8. Remove from oven. Cool slightly and then frost with Caramel Frosting.

9. To prepare Frosting, heat butter, milk, brown sugar, and vanilla in a medium-sized saucepan over low heat, stirring until smooth.

10. Remove from heat and add confectioners sugar. Stir until very smooth.

11. Keep frosting warm, and frost each tray of Cookies as soon as they can be handled.

Sally Anne's

Anna Marie Groff
ANNA MARIE GROFF'S FLOWERS

Makes about 3 dozen cookies ❧ *Prep. Time: 20 minutes*
Chilling Time: overnight, or 8 hours ❧ *Baking Time: 7–8 minutes per baking sheet*

1 cup sugar

1 cup brown sugar

1½ cups shortening

3 eggs

4½ cups flour

1 tsp. baking soda

1 tsp. baking powder

¼–½ tsp. cinnamon

1 cup English walnuts, *or* pecans, finely chopped

1 tsp. vanilla

NOTE

This makes a light, delicate cookie.

1. In a large electric mixing bowl, cream sugars and shortening together.

2. When well blended, beat in eggs one at a time.

3. In a separate bowl, mix flour, baking soda, baking powder, and cinnamon together.

4. Add gradually to creamed mixture, beating well after each addition. (The dough will be quite stiff.) Fold in nuts and vanilla.

5. Grease your hands lightly. Then form dough into 3 rolls. If the dough won't cooperate, refrigerate it until chilled through.

6. Place rolls on a baking sheet or in a baking pan. Cover and refrigerate overnight, or for at least 8 hours.

7. When ready to bake, slice each roll into thin cookies. Place on lightly greased baking sheets, about 1½" apart.

8. Bake at 325° for 7–8 minutes per baking sheet.

Ka'ek wa Ma'Moul

Omar Saif

SAIF'S MIDDLE EASTERN FOODS

Makes about 70 cookies ❧ *Prep Time: 1 hour*
Standing Time: 8½ hours, or overnight ❧ *Baking Time: 8–10 minutes per baking sheet*

2¼ lbs. semolina flour

1 tsp. mahleb (ground sour
cherry pits)

½ tsp. gum Arabic

¼ cup sugar

1½ cups clarified butter

¼ cup vegetable oil

orange blossom water, *divided*

1.1 lbs. ground walnuts

sugar

cinnamon

1.1 lbs. pitted dates

vegetable oil

1 tsp. instant yeast

confectioners sugar

NOTE

*Making these cookies is
usually an extended-
family event. Women
gather to make the sweets
together. Children are often
given the job of pinching
the cookies with tweezers.*

1. Place semolina in deep mixing bowl. Stir in
   the mahleb, gum Arabic, and sugar until well
   mixed.

2. Pour butter, oil, and a few drops orange
   blossom water over dry ingredients. Mix
   thoroughly.

3. Cover dough and let stand overnight.

4. Grind walnuts fine. Stir in sugar and
   cinnamon to taste. Add a bit of orange
   blossom water. Set aside.

5. Grind dates in a meat grinder until they form
   a paste. Mix with some cinnamon to taste
   and some vegetable oil to hold the mixture
   together firmly.

6. Shape date mixture into ropes about ⅜" thick.
   Place ropes on a baking sheet. Cover tightly
   and refrigerate.

7. The next day, stir yeast into semolina dough.

8. Mix a bit of room-temperature water into
   dough, enough to create a soft, pliable dough.

9. Cover dough and set in a warm place for
   30 minutes.

10. Knead dough again, adding a bit more water
    if needed to make it soft and workable.

11. To make the Ka'ek, pinch off bits of dough, each about the size of a walnut. Flatten each piece. Cut a piece of the date rope and place it in the center of the flattened dough. Bring the dough up around the date piece and form into a somewhat flattened ball.

12. Pinch the outer edge of the ball, the whole way around, with a tweezers to form a grooved and ragged edge, depicting the crown of thorns. Be careful not to cut so deeply that you expose the date filling.

13. Place each finished Ka'ek cookie on a baking sheet.

14. To make the Ma'Moul, pinch off bits of dough, each about the size of a small walnut. Form into balls.

15. Then poke your finger into each ball. Fill each cookie's indentation with a small portion of the nut mixture.

16. Pinch shut and re-shape into a dome-shaped ball.

17. Snip the outer edge of each cookie with a tweezers, again being careful not to cut too deeply so that the nut filling is exposed. The ragged edge of these balls depict a sponge.

18. Place on baking sheets.

19. Preheat oven to 500°. Bake cookies 8–10 minutes per baking sheet, or until just golden.

20. Cool completely on baking trays. Then store in an airtight container.

21. Just before serving, dust with confectioners sugar.

These two cookies—one with date filling and the other with walnut filling—are traditional Palestinian sweets, made for Easter and other feasts and holidays. The flatter, more round cookies (the Ka'ek) are intended to represent the crown of thorns that Jesus wore on his head at the cross. The dome-shaped cookies (the Ma'Moul) represent the sponge used to moisten Jesus' parched lips while on the cross.

Pecan Bars

Wendy Hess
WENDY JO'S HOMEMADE

Makes 9–12 servings
Prep. Time: 20–25 minutes ❧ *Baking Time: 35–40minutes* ❧ *Cooling Time: 30 minutes*

Shortbread:
¾ stick (6 Tbsp.) softened butter
2 cups flour
½ cup brown sugar
¾ tsp. salt

Top Layer:
1 stick (8 Tbsp.) butter
1 cup brown sugar
⅓ cup (generous) honey
¼ cup heavy whipping cream
2 cups pecans, chopped

1. Make the Shortbread by mixing 6 Tbsp. butter, flour, brown sugar, and salt until crumbly.

2. Press into a 9" × 9" baking pan.

3. Bake at 350° for 18 minutes.

4. Meanwhile, begin preparing Top Layer by melting 1 stick butter in saucepan over medium-low heat.

5. Add brown sugar, honey, and heavy cream. Mix well.

6. Add pecans, stirring occasionally.

7. Remove Shortbread from oven. Spoon nut mixture on top. Using a spatula, spread gently and evenly over the Shortbread.

8. Return to oven and bake 15–18 minutes more, or until lightly browned.

9. Cool. Then cut into 9 or 12 squares.

French Cream Mint Bars

Anna Mary Glick
LETTUCE TOSS SALAD

Arlene Leaman
S. CLYDE WEAVER, INC.

Makes about 20 servings

Prep. Time: 15–30 minutes ❧ Baking Time: 25 minutes ❧ Freezing Time: 2–3 hours

First Chocolate Layer:
1 cup sugar
1 stick (8 Tbsp.) butter, softened
4 eggs
2 cups chocolate syrup
1 cup bread flour
½ tsp. baking powder

Mint Cream Center:
1 stick (8 Tbsp.) butter, softened
2 cups confectioners sugar
1 Tbsp. milk
½ tsp. peppermint extract
2–3 drops green food coloring, *optional*

Chocolate Topping:
2 cups chocolate chips
1 stick (8 Tbsp.) butter

VARIATION

In the Mint Cream Center, you can substitute 2 Tbsp. green crème de menthe extract in place of the milk, peppermint extract, and green food coloring.

—ARLENE LEAMAN,
S. Clyde Weaver, Inc.

1. In a large electric mixer bowl, cream 1 cup sugar and 1 stick butter together. When well blended, mix in eggs.

2. When well blended, mix in syrup.

3. Then mix in flour and baking powder until thoroughly blended.

4. Spread dough in greased 11" × 15" jelly-roll pan.

5. Bake at 350° for 25 minutes.

6. Cool.

7. Meanwhile, beat together Mint Cream Center ingredients in a large electric mixer bowl until smooth and creamy.

8. Spread over completely cooled crust.

9. Freeze for several hours until thoroughly chilled and firm.

10. In a microwave-safe bowl, melt chocolate chips and butter together to make Topping. Microwave on High for 1 minute, or until chips and butter melt when stirred.

11. Spread Topping over chilled Bars. Cover and chill another hour before cutting into bars and serving.

12. Cut into individual Bars and serve.

Frosted Banana Bars

Donna Shenk
SHENK'S POULTRY

Makes 18–20 servings
Prep. Time: 20 minutes ❦ *Baking Time: 25 minutes*

Cake:

1 stick (8 Tbsp.) butter, softened

2 cups sugar

3 eggs

1½ cups (3 medium) mashed bananas

1 tsp. vanilla

2 cups flour

1 tsp. baking soda

pinch of salt

Frosting:

1 stick (8 Tbsp.) butter, softened

8-oz. pkg. cream cheese, softened

4 cups confectioners sugar

2 tsp. vanilla

1. Prepare Cake by creaming butter and sugar together in a large electric mixing bowl.

2. Beat in eggs, bananas, and vanilla.

3. In a separate mixing bowl, combine flour, baking soda, and salt.

4. Stir into creamed ingredients, mixing well.

5. Pour into a greased 10" × 15" baking pan.

6. Bake at 350° for 25 minutes, or until tester inserted in center of cake comes out clean.

7. Cool.

8. While bars are cooling, prepare Frosting by creaming butter and cream cheese together in an electric mixing bowl.

9. Gradually add confectioners sugar and vanilla, beating until thoroughly combined.

10. Spread over cooled bars.

11. Cut into 15–20 bars. Store leftovers in refrigerator.

Frosted Peanut Butter Bars

Margie Shaffer
S. CLYDE WEAVER, INC.

Makes 30 servings

Prep. Time: 15-20 minutes ❧ Baking Time: 16-20 minutes ❧ Cooling Time: 1 hour

Bars:

½ cup peanut butter

⅓ cup (5⅓ Tbsp.) butter, softened

1½ cups packed brown sugar

2 eggs

1 tsp. vanilla

1½ cups flour

1½ tsp. baking powder

½ tsp. salt

¼ cup milk

Frosting:

⅔ cup peanut butter

½ cup shortening

4 cups confectioners sugar

⅓–½ cup milk

¼ cup chocolate chips for drizzling, *optional*

VARIATION

To turn this into a traditional cake, spoon the batter in Step 5 into a 9"×13" baking pan. Baking time may need to increase slightly. You'll likely have fewer servings, depending on the size of the pieces.

1. To make the Bars, cream together peanut butter, butter, and brown sugar in an electric mixer bowl.

2. Beat in eggs and vanilla.

3. In a medium-sized bowl, combine flour, baking powder, and salt.

4. Add alternately with milk to creamed mixture. Mix well.

5. Spread into greased 10"×15" baking pan.

6. Bake at 350° for 16–20 minutes, or until toothpick inserted in center comes out clean.

7. Cool to room temperature.

8. To make Frosting, combine peanut butter, shortening, and confectioners sugar in an electric mixer bowl.

9. Gradually add milk until Frosting reaches spreading consistency. Frost cake.

10. Place chocolate chips in microwave-safe dish. Melt on high for 20–30 seconds, or until chips turn to liquid when stirred.

11. Drizzle chocolate over frosted bars.

Granola Bars

Anna Mary Glick
LETTUCE TOSS SALAD

Makes 20 servings
Prep. Time: 15 minutes ✽ *Cooking Time: 10–15 minutes*

4 cups dry quick oats
½ cup brown sugar, packed
1½ cups nuts, chopped
1 tsp. salt
1 cup chocolate chips
1 cup flaked coconut
1½ sticks (12 Tbsp.) butter, melted
½ cup peanut butter
1 tsp. vanilla
½ cup honey

1. Preheat oven to 375°.

2. Combine dry quick oats, brown sugar, nuts, salt, chocolate chips, and flaked coconut in a large mixing bowl.

3. In a separate bowl, mix melted butter, peanut butter, vanilla, and honey together. When smooth, stir into dry ingredients.

4. Press mixture into lightly greased 10"×15" baking pan with sides.

5. Bake 10–15 minutes, or until golden brown and bubbly.

6. When partially cooled, cut into bars. Allow to cool completely before removing from pan.

7. Serve immediately, or store in airtight container.

Easy One-Bowl Pumpkin Bars

Ruth Thomas
THOMAS PRODUCE

Makes 24 servings

Prep. Time: 18–20 minutes ❧ *Baking Time: 30–35 minutes* ❧ *Cooling Time: 30 minutes*

Bars:

2 cups flour

2 cups sugar

2 cups cooked pumpkin, mashed,
or 15½-oz. can pumpkin

1 cup vegetable oil

4 eggs

2 tsp. baking powder

1 tsp. baking soda

1 tsp. cinnamon

½ tsp. salt

Cream Cheese Frosting:

1 stick (8 Tbsp.) butter, softened

8-oz. pkg. cream cheese, softened

2 cups confectioners sugar

1 tsp. vanilla

1. In large electric mixer bowl, beat together all ingredients for Bars until texture is smooth.

2. Pour into a greased 10" × 13" jelly-roll pan.

3. Bake at 350° for 30–35 minutes, or until center is set.

4. Cool completely.

5. While bars are cooling, make Cream Cheese Frosting.

6. In a medium-sized electric mixer bowl, beat butter and cream cheese together until soft and creamy.

7. Gradually stir in 2 cups confectioners sugar.

8. Add vanilla, beating well.

9. When Bars are completely cool, spread Frosting over top. Then cut into individual Bars.

Zucchini Brownies

Eugene A. Martin
S. CLYDE WEAVER, INC.

Makes 12–15 servings
Prep. Time: 15–20 minutes   Baking Time: 25–30 minutes

2 cups flour
1½ cups sugar
1½ tsp. baking soda
1 tsp. salt
¼ cup cocoa powder
½ cup chopped nuts
2 cups finely grated zucchini (squeezed dry)
½ cup canola oil
2 tsp. vanilla

1. In a large mixing bowl, mix together flour, sugar, baking soda, salt, cocoa powder, and nuts.

2. Add zucchini, oil, and vanilla. Stir just until moistened.

3. Pour into well greased 9" × 13" baking pan.

4. Bake at 350° for 25–30 minutes.

My Mom's Brownies

Janelle and Kendal Yoder
LETTUCE TOSS SALAD

Makes about 12 servings
Prep. Time: 10–15 minutes   Cooking Time: 30 minutes

1½ cups flour
2 cups sugar
½ cup cocoa powder
½ tsp. salt
¾ cup vegetable oil
4 eggs
2 tsp. vanilla

1. Measure all ingredients into an electric mixing bowl in the order listed.

2. Beat at medium speed for 3 minutes.

3. Pour into a greased 9" × 13" baking pan.

4. Bake at 350° for 30 minutes.

NOTE

I often make this spontaneously before guests come over. It's nearly as easy as a mix but completely homemade.

Rhubarb Sorbet

Betsey Sterenfeld
CENTRAL MARKET CUSTOMER

Makes about 1 quart sorbet ❦ *Prep. Time: 10–15 minutes*
Cooking Time: 5 minutes ❦ *Cooling Time: 2 hours* ❦ *Chilling/Freezing Time: about 3 hours*

2 lbs. rhubarb

1 cup water

1 cup raw sugar

¼ cup honey

zest from 1 orange

2 tsp. fresh ginger, grated, *optional* *

3 Tbsp. Aperol, an Italian aperitif

*NOTE

Since ginger has a bold taste, you may want to reduce the amount called for, or eliminate it if you are doubtful about it.

1. Cut rhubarb into ½" pieces.

2. Place rhubarb, water, sugar, honey, orange zest, and, if you wish, ginger in a heavy, medium-sized saucepan.

3. Bring to boil. Reduce heat. Cover and simmer about 5 minutes, or until rhubarb is tender and cooked through.

4. Remove from heat and let cool to room temperature.

5. Purée cooked rhubarb mixture and Aperol in blender or food processor until smooth.

6. Chill mixture thoroughly.

7. Freeze in ice-cream maker according to manufacturer's instructions.

TIPS

1. *Let sorbet soften 15–20 minutes before serving.*

2. *Crumbled cookies, especially Italian almond macaroons, are great go-alongs with this recipe.*

Mexican Fried Ice Cream

Carl Charles

S. CLYDE WEAVER, INC.

Makes 20 servings

Thawing Time: 30 minutes ❧ *Prep. Time: 20–30 minutes* ❧ *Freezing Time: 5 hours*

1½ quarts vanilla bean ice cream

1½ quarts butter pecan ice cream

8-oz. container frozen whipped topping, thawed

2 tsp. cinnamon

1 stick (8 Tbsp.) butter

1 cup sugar

3 cups crushed cornflakes

honey

cinnamon

1. Thaw ice cream for 30 minutes.

2. In a large bowl, mix 2 ice creams together. Fold in whipped topping and cinnamon until well blended.

3. Spread in 9" × 13" pan.

4. Melt butter and sugar in medium-sized skillet.

5. Add crushed cornflakes to butter/sugar mixture. Sauté about 1½ minutes, stirring continually.

6. Pour over ice cream.

7. Drizzle with honey and sprinkle extra cinnamon on top.

8. Freeze for 5 hours.

9. Cut into squares. Serve with extra honey for drizzling over individual servings.

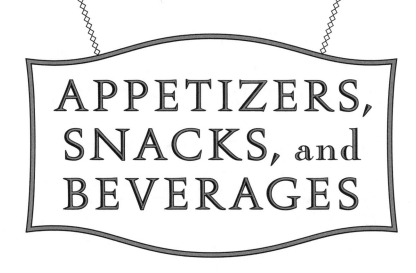

APPETIZERS, SNACKS, and BEVERAGES

Salami Canapes

Sally Delgiorno
DELGIORNO'S ITALIAN SPECIALTIES

Makes: 4–6 servings
Prep. Time: 10 minutes ❧ *Broiling Time: 5 minutes or so*

½ cup chopped black olives

¾ cup grated Parmesan cheese

½ lb. hard, or Genoa, salami, chopped fine

mayonnaise

party-sized pumpernickel *or* rye bread slices, *or* French *or* Italian baguette slices

shredded sharp, *or* mozzarella, cheese

1. In a medium-sized bowl, mix together black olives, Parmesan cheese, and salami.

2. Stir in just enough mayonnaise to allow mixture to stick together.

3. Spread on small slices of bread (a variety looks appealing).

4. Top with cheese.

5. Broil until cheese melts and is bubbly.

Nancy's Olive Tapenade

Nancy Shenk
SPRING GLEN

Makes 10-12 servings
Prep. Time: 20 minutes ❧ *Chilling Time: overnight, or 8 hours*

12 ozs. pitted ripe olives
12 ozs. pickled red peppers
2 Tbsp. olive oil
2 Tbsp. red wine vinegar

1. Drain olives and peppers. Chop fine. (It's faster to use a food processor, but if you do, don't turn the ingredients into paste!)

2. Transfer to mixing bowl.

3. Stir in olive oil and red wine vinegar.

4. Cover and refrigerate overnight to allow flavors to blend.

5. Serve with crackers or bagel chips.

Belgian Endive and Chèvre Appetizer

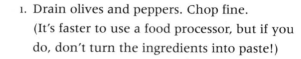

Sam Neff
S. CLYDE WEAVER, INC.

Makes 8-10 servings
Prep. Time: 30 minutes ❧ *Cooking Time: 5 minutes*

⅓ cup English walnuts, finely chopped, *divided*
2 Tbsp. butter
8 ozs. goat's milk cheese (chèvre), preferably from a 1 kilo log
1–2 Tbsp. walnut oil
1–2 Tbsp. lemon juice
5 heads Belgian endive (to yield 50 well-shaped leaves *or* spears)
fresh red pepper strips for garnish

1. Sauté English walnuts in butter and brown to your taste. Set aside.

2. Mix goat's milk cheese with walnut oil and lemon juice. If mixture is of spreading consistency, add ¾ of the walnuts. If mixture is too firm, add a bit more walnut oil and lemon juice.

3. Spread cheese mixture on endive leaves and arrange in a sunburst pattern on a tray or dish. Sprinkle with remaining walnuts.

4. Use fresh red pepper strips to add color.

Fresh Asparagus Wrapped with Prosciutto or Westphalian Ham

Sam Neff
S. CLYDE WEAVER, INC.

2 spears = 1 serving ❧ *Prep. Time: 2-3 minutes* ❧ *Cooking Time: 2 minutes*

asparagus
prosciutto *or* Westphalian ham

1. Blanch asparagus. Immerse it in ice water so it doesn't get too soft.

2. Wrap spears of asparagus with half a slice of prosciutto or Westphalian ham.

Stuffed Jalapeño Peppers

Deb Becker
CENTRAL MARKET CUSTOMER

Makes 6-8 servings ❧ *Prep. Time: 45-60 minutes* ❧ *Cooking Time: 30 minutes*

8-oz. pkg. cream cheese, softened

8 ozs. shredded sharp cheddar cheese

¼ cup mayonnaise

25 fresh jalapeño peppers, halved lengthwise and seeded

2 eggs, beaten

½ cup milk

1½–2 cups crushed cornflake crumbs

1. Preheat oven to 350°.

2. Lightly grease a medium-sized baking sheet.

3. In a medium-sized bowl, mix together cream cheese, cheddar cheese, and mayonnaise.

4. Stuff jalapeño halves with mixture.

5. Whisk together eggs and milk in a small bowl.

6. Dip each stuffed jalapeño half into the egg mixture.

7. Roll in cornflake crumbs to coat.

8. Arrange in a single layer on prepared baking sheet. Spoon any loose/leftover crumbs over stuffed peppers on baking sheet.

9. Bake 30 minutes, or until filling is bubbly and lightly browned.

TIP

These freeze well for a great winter-time treat!

Strawberry, Orange, and Avocado Salsa

Betsey Sterenfeld
CENTRAL MARKET CUSTOMER

Makes 4 servings
Prep. Time: 10–15 minutes

2 pints strawberries
2 small oranges
1 Tbsp. sugar
1 ripe avocado, cubed
1 lemon, zested and juiced
kosher salt
freshly ground black pepper

1. Stem and cut strawberries into ¼"-thick slices. Place in mixing bowl.

2. Cut all peel and pith off oranges. Working over strawberry bowl to catch orange juice, cut between membranes, releasing orange segments into bowl.

3. Squeeze juice from orange peels and membranes into same bowl.

4. Sprinkle with sugar and mix gently.

5. Place cubed avocado in bowl with fruit.

6. Place lemon zest and juice over mixture. Mix gently.

7. Season to taste with salt and pepper.

8. Serve soon. The Salsa is a good accompaniment to grilled meats or veggies, and to tacos and Latin food.

TIPS

1. *Refreshing as part of a brunch.*

2. *Kids love to make and eat it.*

3. *Not a good make-ahead recipe.*

Mango Salsa

Janelle Glick
LANCASTER GENERAL WELLNESS PARTNERSHIP

Makes about 1⅓ cups, or about 4 servings
Prep. Time: 15 minutes, including cutting the mango Standing Time: 15 minutes

1 ripe mango, diced (1½ cups)
¼ cup finely chopped red onion
2 Tbsp. lime juice
2 Tbsp. rice vinegar
1 Tbsp. chopped fresh cilantro

1. Combine mango cubes, onion, lime juice, vinegar, and cilantro in medium bowl.

2. Let stand 15 minutes.

3. Stir before serving.

4. Serve with taco or bagel chips

TIP FOR CUTTING A MANGO

1. *Slice both ends off mango, revealing long, slender seed inside. Set fruit upright on work surface. Remove skin with a sharp knife.*

2. *With the seed perpendicular to you, slice the fruit from both sides of the seed, yielding two large pieces.*

3. *Turn the seed parallel to you and slice the two smaller pieces of fruit from each side.*

4. *Cut fruit into small cubes.*

Small-Batch Fresh Tomato Salsa

Janelle Glick

LANCASTER GENERAL WELLNESS PARTNERSHIP

Makes 1½ cups
Prep. Time: 15 minutes

2 medium-sized tomatoes

1–2 jalapeño peppers, depending on your tolerance for "heat"

2 Tbsp. finely chopped red onion

2 Tbsp. chopped fresh cilantro, *or* fresh parsley

1 clove garlic, minced

1–2 tsp. lemon juice

¼ tsp. salt

1. Seed and dice tomatoes. Place in mixing bowl.

2. Seed and mince jalapeño peppers. Add to mixing bowl.

3. Combine in mixing bowl with tomatoes and peppers: onion, cilantro, garlic, lemon juice, and salt.

4. Serve within an hour.

Fresh Garden Salsa

Dawn Mellinger

ROHRER FAMILY FARM

Makes about 5¾ cups
Prep. Time: 25 minutes   Chilling Time: overnight, or 8 hours

15-oz. can diced tomatoes with green chilies, undrained

8 Roma tomatoes, chopped

1 large garlic clove, minced

1 large onion, chopped fine

half a bell pepper, chopped

1–2 chopped jalapeño peppers, *optional*

2 tsp. fresh cilantro, finely chopped

1 tsp. salt

1½ Tbsp. white, *or* red wine, vinegar

1. Pour can of diced tomatoes into food processor. Purée.

2. Pour puréed tomatoes into mixing bowl. Add other chopped or minced ingredients.

3. Stir in salt and vinegar.

4. Mix together.

5. Cover and refrigerate overnight before serving.

Taste of the Ozarks Homemade Salsa

Pamela Brenner
LANCASTER JUICE CO.

Makes approximately 14 pints
Prep. Time: 30–60 minutes ❦ Cooking Time: 2 hours

6 quarts chopped fresh tomatoes, slightly drained

5–6 medium-sized onions, chopped

6–12 jalapeño peppers, chopped, depending on your "heat" preference

1 bulb garlic, finely chopped, *or* 3 heaping Tbsp. minced garlic

10 medium-sized green, red, yellow, *or* mixture of, bell peppers, coarsely chopped

12-oz. can tomato paste

1½ tsp. salt

1 Tbsp. pepper

1½ cups white vinegar

2 envelopes salsa seasoning (Mrs. Wages is best)

1. Mix all ingredients in a large stockpot. Bring to boil.

2. Simmer 2 hours.

3. Fill canning jars and cap with lids and rings.

4. Process according to canning equipment directions.

5. Serve with corn chips or on fresh homemade macaroni and cheese.

TIPS

1. *I chop all the vegetables in a food processor to save time.*

2. *I almost never can this salsa. Instead, I refrigerate it and then use it fast and also give it away!*

3. *We make this a family project when vegetables can be brought fresh from the garden or bought fresh on Market. We work outside with the food processor to save the mess in the kitchen. We keep chips nearby!*

Apple Chutney

Janelle Glick

LANCASTER GENERAL WELLNESS PARTNERSHIP

Makes 2 cups

Prep. Time: 15 minutes ❦ *Cooking Time: 60 minutes* ❦ *Cooling Time: 30 minutes*

2 large tart cooking apples
(Granny Smith variety works well)

½ cup chopped onion

¼ cup red wine vinegar

¼ cup brown sugar

1 Tbsp. grated orange peel

1 Tbsp. grated fresh ginger

½ tsp. allspice

1. Peel, core, and chop apples.

2. Combine apples, onions, vinegar, brown sugar, orange peel, fresh ginger, and allspice in medium saucepan. Stir well.

3. Bring to boil. Reduce heat and simmer, covered, for 50 minutes.

4. Uncover and simmer over low heat for a few more minutes to cook off excess liquid. Let cool.

5. Cover and refrigerate for up to two weeks.

6. Serve on a cheese plate as a dip, or with crackers. Or serve as a complement to roast pork or burgers (see page 87).

Pineapple Cheese Dip

Nancy Shenk
SPRING GLEN

Makes about 2 cups
Prep. Time: 15 minutes ✽ *Chilling Time: 3–4 hours*

¾ cup (about 3 ozs.) sharp cheddar cheese, shredded

½ cup green and red peppers, finely chopped

8-oz. can crushed pineapples in juice, well-drained

8-oz. pkg. Neufchâtel cream cheese, softened

1. Combine all ingredients in a medium-sized bowl.

2. Cover and chill thoroughly.

3. Serve with crackers.

NOTE
_____

I take this to the shore every year, and we snack on it all week.

Taco Dip

Sally Delgiorno
DELGIORNO'S ITALIAN SPECIALTIES

Serves a crowd (makes about 11 cups)
Prep. Time: 20 minutes

2 8-oz. pkgs. cream cheese, softened

16 ozs. sour cream

1 envelope taco seasoning mix

about 3 cups shredded lettuce

2 medium-sized tomatoes, chopped

1 medium-sized onion, chopped, *or* about ½–¾ cup green onions, sliced

2 cups shredded mozzarella cheese

nacho chips

1. In a good-sized bowl, beat cream cheese until smooth. Fold in sour cream until well blended.

2. Add taco seasoning mix and blend well.

3. Spread on bottom of 9" × 13" baking dish.

4. Layer lettuce, tomatoes, and onions evenly over cream-cheese mixture.

5. Sprinkle shredded cheese overtop.

6. Serve with nacho chips for dipping.

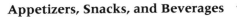

Chesapeake Bay Party Nuts

Susan Stoeckl
SUSAN'S SECRET GARDEN

Makes 4 cups
Prep. Time: 10 minutes ❧ *Baking Time: 30 minutes* ❧ *Cooling Time: 10 minutes*

2 Tbsp. butter, melted

2 tsp. Old Bay seasoning

2 Tbsp. Worcestershire sauce

½ tsp. garlic powder

¼–½ tsp. hot sauce, depending upon your tolerence for "heat"

2 cups pecans

2 cups halved, *or* whole, almonds

1. In a good-sized mixing bowl, stir together melted butter, Old Bay seasoning, Worcestershire sauce, garlic powder, and hot sauce.

2. Add nuts, tossing to coat.

3. Place nuts on foil-lined 10" × 15" baking pan with sides.

4. Bake at 300° for 30 minutes. Stir twice during the baking time.

5. Cool completely. Serve, or store in an airtight container.

Mints

Anna Marie Groff
ANNA MARIE GROFF'S FLOWERS

Makes about 12 dozen tiny mints
Prep. Time: 1¼ hours

half an 8-oz. pkg. cream cheese, softened

3 drops flavoring (peppermint, wintergreen, *or* spearmint oil)

1 lb. confectioners sugar

1. Place softened cream cheese and 3 drops flavoring in small bowl of electric mixer. Cream together until smooth.

2. Gradually add sugar until workable dough forms.

3. Using your hands, form into tiny balls about the size of dinner mints.

4. Cover a large flat surface with waxed paper. Place balls on waxed paper.

5 Press fork on tops to flatten.

6. Store in airtight containers. Refrigerate until ready to serve.

Chocolate Peanut Butter Snack

Sharon Glick
MAPLEHOFE DAIRY

Prep. Time: 15 minutes
Chilling Time: 1 hour

1 lb. white coating chocolate
½ cup peanut butter
1 cup chocolate chips

1. Place white coating chocolate in 4-cup microwave-safe bowl. Microwave on high 2 minutes. Stir. Microwave on high another minute. Stir. Microwave on high for 30-second intervals until chocolate is smooth when stirred.

2. Stir in peanut butter.

3. Spread on a greased baking sheet with low sides.

4. Place chocolate chips in microwave-safe bowl. Microwave on high 1 minute. Stir. Microwave on high for 30 seconds. Stir. If not smooth when stirred, microwave another 30 seconds on high. Stir until smooth.

5. Pour over white chocolate.

6. Marble with table knife.

7. Refrigerate for 1 hour.

8. Break into pieces when firm.

TIP

I like to use this as a little gift at the holidays or as a thinking-of-you gift anytime. You can place the candy in a canning jar or little box.

Spicy Rice Balls

NARAI THAI CUISINE

Makes 15-20 balls
Prep. Time: 10 minutes ❦ Cooking Time: 25 minutes

2 cups finely chopped cooked chicken

3 cups cooked jasmine rice

2 Tbsp. chopped fresh lemon grass

1 Tbsp. salt

1 tsp. red pepper

1 cup flaked coconut

1 egg

3" oil

1. In a good-sized bowl, mix finely chopped chicken with cooked rice.

2. Add chopped lemon grass, salt, and red pepper. Mix well.

3. Add coconut flakes and roll into small balls.

4. Beat egg.

5. Dip balls into egg. Deep-fry in 3" *hot* oil until golden.

TIP
_____

It is very important that the oil be hot!

No person shall keep any horse, cart, carriage, wagon, wheel-barrow, or other vehicle in the avenues around the Market House any longer than may be necessary to unload the same and place their goods on the stalls; and all persons occupying stands out of the Market House, and selling from wagons and other vehicles, shall back their vehicles against the curb stone and remove their horses as soon as possible.

— MARKET RULES, 1889

Frozen Fruit

Joanne Warfel
S. CLYDE WEAVER, INC.

Makes 25 servings

Prep. Time: 1 hour ❦ Cooking Time: 10 minutes ❦ Cooling Time: 15 minutes

1 small watermelon, cubed *or* balled

1 cantaloupe, cubed *or* balled

half a honeydew, cubed *or* balled

2 lbs. seedless grapes

2 lbs. peaches, sliced

¾ lb. blueberries

Syrup:

2 cups sugar

1 quart water

6-oz. can orange juice concentrate

6-oz. can lemonade concentrate

1. Prepare syrup by combining sugar and water in a saucepan.

2. Bring to a boil. Stir frequently to make sure sugar is dissolved and to prevent scorching.

3. Stir in orange juice and lemonade concentrates.

4. Cool fully.

5. Combine fruits in large bowl.

6. Stir in cooled juice and freeze in pint-size or quart-size containers.

TIP

I like to serve this as a refreshing appetizer. I thaw it until it's slushy, and then top individual servings with orange or lime sherbet.

Fruit Smoothie

Sara Neilon
CENTRAL MARKET CUSTOMER

Makes 3-4 servings
Prep. Time: 5-10 minutes

1½ cups flavored yogurt of your choice (vanilla, lemon, or your preference)

2 bananas, peeled

1 orange, peeled, and membranes between sections removed

1 cup strawberries, stemmed and sliced

½ cup blueberries

2–3 Tbsp. flax oil, *optional*

1. Place yogurt, all the fruit, and flax oil if you wish in blender.

2. Blend until smooth.

3. Serve immediately.

TIP

You can use any fruit, especially very ripe fruit such as brown bananas, that might not otherwise be eaten. The variety is endless. You can also hide fruits that children may not eat separately.

Golden Punch for a Party

Joanne Warfel
S. CLYDE WEAVER, INC.

Makes 80 servings
Prep. Time: 15 minutes

3 6-oz. cans frozen lemonade concentrate

3 6-oz. cans frozen orange juice concentrate

46-oz. can grapefruit juice

46-oz. can pineapple juice

5 cups sugar

1 liter, or more, ginger ale, *or* 7 Up

water to make 5 gallons Punch

ice cubes

1. In a very large bowl or clean bucket, combine first 5 ingredients to make base. Stir until well mixed.

2. Add ginger ale or 7 Up. Stir well.

3. Add water to make 5 gallons. Stir well.

4. Add ice to individual glasses when ready to serve. Pour Punch over ice.

Rhubarb Punch

Ruth Thomas
THOMAS PRODUCE

Makes 6–8 servings
Prep. Time: 15 minutes ❧ Cooking Time: 10 minutes ❧ Cooling Time: 2 hours

4 cups water

1–1¼ cups sugar, depending on your taste preference

2 cups rhubarb, diced

juice of 1 lemon

½ cup orange juice

½ cup ginger ale

ice cubes

1. Place water and sugar in good-sized saucepan and stir until sugar is nearly dissolved. Stir in diced rhubarb.

2. Cover and bring mixture to boil. Tilt lid and allow mixture to boil 2 minutes.

3. Strain and cool to room temperature.

4. Add lemon juice, orange juice, and ginger ale.

5. Stir well.

6. Pour over ice cubes and serve.

My sister Miriam and I drove to market as teenagers in the 1930s. My mother, father, Miriam, and I picked berries, peas, and vegetables in season, and we also dressed five or six chickens the morning before we went to market, which opened at 2 p.m.

We always had a few baskets of eggs which we sold and put in paper bags, because there weren't any egg cartons. We bunched rhubarb, onions, etc. with string because nobody had rubber bands.

We parked at Hager's parking lot for 25 cents a day. There was a gas pump there, and, if we bought gas, parking was free.

— HELEN A. THOMAS, Thomas Produce

Mocha Punch – Two Variations!
Variation #1

Stephanie Shelly
S. CLYDE WEAVER, INC.

Makes 8-10 servings
Cooking Time 10 minutes ❦ Chilling Time: overnight, or 8 hours

6 cups boiling water

¼ cup instant coffee granules, regular *or* decaf

1 cup sugar

4 cups milk

1½ tsp. vanilla

⅓ cup chocolate syrup

½ gallon vanilla ice cream

1. The day before (or at least 8 hours before) serving Punch, bring water to boil in saucepan.

2. Add instant coffee and sugar. Stir to dissolve.

3. Add milk, vanilla, and chocolate syrup. Mix well.

4. Refrigerate mixture overnight, or at least 8 hours.

5. Just before serving, stir in ice cream.

NOTE
_____

This makes a great summertime, cool drink for coffee-lovers.

Variation #2

Margie Shaffer
S. CLYDE WEAVER, INC.

Makes 16-20 servings (about 5 quarts)
Cooking Time: 15 minutes ❦ Chilling Time: at least 4 hours

1½ quarts water

½ cup powdered chocolate drink mix

½ cup sugar

¼ cup instant coffee granules, regular *or* decaf

1. Bring water to a boil in a good-sized saucepan.

2. Remove from heat and stir in drink mix, sugar, and coffee granules until dissolved.

3. Refrigerate mixture at least 4 hours.

½ gallon vanilla ice cream

½ gallon chocolate ice cream

frozen whipped topping, thawed, *optional*

chocolate curls, *optional*

4. Thirty minutes before serving, pour into punch bowl and add ice cream by the spoonful.

5. Stir until partially melted.

6. If you wish, garnish individual servings with whipped topping and/or chocolate curls.

Iced Coffee

Barbara Lapp
DUTCH COUNTRY DELI

Makes 4-5 servings
Prep. Time: 5 minutes ❧ *Cooling Time: 1 hour*

Coffee Base:

2 cups boiling water

1½ cups sugar

½ cup instant coffee granules, regular *or* decaf

2 Tbsp. vanilla

To make 1 serving Iced Coffee:

¼ cup coffee base

1 cup milk

1 cup crushed ice

1. Mix all Coffee Base ingredients in saucepan, stirring until all ingredients are dissolved.

2. Cool to room temperature. Store Base in refrigerator.

3. To make individual servings of iced coffee, mix Coffee Base, milk, and ice together in large mug. Serve immediately.

Victorian Eggnog

Janelle and Kendal Yoder
LETTUCE TOSS SALAD

Makes 4-6 servings

Prep. Time: 10 minutes ❧ Cooking Time: 15 minutes ❧ Cooling Time: 10 minutes

2 cups whipping cream
1 cup half-and-half
6 large egg yolks
½ cup sugar
1 tsp. nutmeg, *divided*
6 Tbsp. dry sherry, *optional*

NOTE

We enjoy bringing Victorian Eggnog to our family Christmas gatherings. Everyone always enjoys, or is at least curious enough to sample, the original version of the usually store-bought seasonal beverage.

1. Bring cream and half-and-half to a simmer in a good-sized saucepan.

2. Whisk egg yolks and sugar together in large bowl to blend.

3. Gradually whisk hot cream mixture into yolk mixture.

4. Return everything to saucepan.

5. Stir over medium-low heat until thickened, about 4 minutes (when a path forms behind spoon when stirring). Do not allow mixture to boil.

6. Strain into clean bowl.

7. Stir in ¾ tsp. nutmeg.

8. Allow to cool slightly.

9. Divide eggnog into 6 glasses. Stir 1 Tbsp. sherry into each.

10. Sprinkle each with a pinch of nutmeg.

Index

About The Author

Phyllis Pellman Good is a *New York Times* bestselling author whose books have sold nearly 10 million copies. Good is a native of Lancaster County, Pennsylvania. As a teenager she worked on Central Market, and today as a resident of Lancaster City, she shops on Market regularly.

Good authored the national #1 bestselling cookbook *Fix-It and Forget-It Cookbook: Feasting with Your Slow Cooker* (with Dawn J. Ranck), which appeared on *The New York Times* bestseller list, as well as the bestseller lists of *USA Today*, *Publishers Weekly*, and *Book Sense*. And she is the author of *Fix-It and Forget-It Lightly: Healthy, Low-Fat Recipes for Your Slow Cooker*, which has also appeared on *The New York Times* bestseller list. In addition, Good authored four other books in the series, including *Fix-It and Forget-It Diabetic Cookbook: Slow-Cooker Favorites to Include Everyone* (with the American Diabetes Association).

Good is also the author of the *Fix-It and Enjoy-It* series, a "cousin" series to the phenomenally successful *Fix-It and Forget-It* cookbooks. There are four books in that series, including the flagship book, *Fix-It and Enjoy-It Cookbook: All-Purpose, Welcome-Home Recipes*, which appeared on *The New York Times* bestseller list, and *Fix-It and Enjoy-It Healthy Cookbook: 400 Great Stove-Top and Oven Recipes* (with nutritional expertise from Mayo Clinic).

Phyllis Pellman Good is Executive Editor at Good Books. (Good Books has published hundreds of titles by more than 135 authors.) She received her B.A. and M.A. in English from New York University. She and her husband, Merle are the parents of two young-adult daughters.

For a complete listing of books by Phyllis Pellman Good, as well as excerpts and reviews, visit www.Fix-ItandForget-It.com or www.GoodBooks.com.